KAROL NIELSEN

BLACK ELEPHANTS

a memoir

D0006561

University of Nebraska Press | Lincoln & London

© 2011 by Karol Nielsen. Acknowledgments for the
use of copyrighted material appear on pages 218–19,
which constitute an extension of the copyright page.
All rights reserved. Manufactured in the United
States of America.

♾

Library of Congress Cataloging-in-Publication Data
Nielsen, Karol.
Black elephants : a memoir / Karol Nielsen.
   p. cm.
Includes bibliographical references.
ISBN 978-0-8032-3537-3 (pbk.: alk. paper)
1. Nielsen, Karol. 2. Man-woman relationships—
Israel. 3. Persian Gulf War, 1991—Israel. I. Title.
HQ801.N54 2011
306.84'5092—dc22
[B]   2011011330

Set in Chaparal Pro by Shirley Thornton.
Designed by A. Shahan.

For my father,
who taught me how
to run hills.

For my mother,
who taught me how
to endure valleys.

For my nephew,
who taught me how
to love.

Let everything happen
to you: beauty and terror.
Just keep going.
No feeling is final.

RANIER MARIA RILKE

Contents

A Note on Names

I have changed some names to
protect the privacy of the people
in the memoir, including Aviv's. I
chose that name because his mother
had wanted to name him Aviv, the
Hebrew word for "spring."

BLACK
ELEPHANTS

1

The New Zealand Sheep
Farmer and the Recruit

The minivan bumped along hills that hugged Lake Titicaca. Haze made the water look silver. I sat behind Dirk, a German traveler with a ponytail. It hung to the middle of his back, streaked bronze from the South American sun. He wore dusty jeans and a tank top that skimmed his torso. Dirk was one of those hard-core travelers, the kind I'd met along the way, who took regular trips through Latin America, Africa, and the Far East. They seemed so worldly, and despite the army tanks, tear gas, and guns I'd seen during my year as a writer for an English-language newspaper in Argentina, I still felt sheltered. I was only beginning to understand the underbelly of the world, something the serious travelers seemed to have understood from birth.

Growing up in Connecticut, I felt the pull of faraway places my father and grandfather had been, places like India, China, and Vietnam. My father fought in the central highlands of Vietnam, as a commissioned officer with the 101st Airborne Division—the Screaming Eagles. After the war, he left the army and became a businessman in New York City. He had a window office in the Chrysler Building. He dressed in suits, ties, and wing-tipped shoes. Secretly, I pictured him trekking through jungle, a Nebraska boy, lean and tall and tan—a Viking in army fatigues. My father never glamorized war, but my mother's father did. He made it sound like an exotic mission, flying over the Himalayas—the camel's hump—from India to China during World War II. He was never Grandfather or Grandpa or anything that sounded old. He was Bobby, the hero who flew the hump. He'd take us to Chinese restaurants and try to impress us by speaking Chinese to the waiters. It worked. I wanted big adventure like Bobby, action like a new recruit.

I wanted to travel the world when I graduated from the University of Pennsylvania, like Marcos, an Argentine friend who'd finished a semester before me. He liked India best. "So many religions!" But I didn't have the money, and my mother said I needed a job. I found one at the *Buenos Aires Herald*, famous for its coverage of Argentina's "dirty war," when thousands disappeared during the military dictatorship. I ended up in Buenos Aires because, as a freshman at Penn, an Argentine student walked up to me and said, "I want to teach you the tango." Jon never taught me the tango, but I got to know most of the Argentines at school. Marcos, his brother Nacho, their cousin Pablo, and their friends, Jon and Martin—Yon and Mar-*teen*—lived in an off-campus row house in West Philadelphia. They called it the Argentine Embassy.

Martin had the classic good looks of an Argentine polo player, and we dated my senior year, but he was two years younger and so studious that he hardly had time for me. A straight-A student at the Wharton School of Business, Martin was in the library night after night until one, two, three, or four in the morning. After we'd broken up, I ran into him in the library and told him I needed an extra semester to finish my thesis.

"Do you have a place to stay?" Martin asked.

"Not yet," I said.

"We have a room."

So during my last months of school, while writing my thesis and an article for the *Penn World Review* on the debt crisis in Brazil and Mexico, I lived in the new Argentine Embassy, farther from campus, on a beaten-down block by a crack house and a gas station. My housemate Patricia was a graduate student who had written for *La Nación*, Argentina's paper of record. She knew that I wanted to travel and write after college, so she said, "Come to Buenos Aires. You can live with me." I went, and for months I lined up cushions from her two small couches and slept on the floor beside her balcony, facing the Rio de la Plata, and then I found a place across the hall. My balcony overlooked a military horse corral, and when my family came for Christmas, my mother went to the balcony and thought, *That's it. I'm not worrying about her anymore!*

This was five years after the end of the military dictatorship, but the mothers of the disappeared still marched in the Plaza de Mayo, holding posters of missing children and grandchildren, stepping over bodies painted on the courtyard like crime-scene markers. Argentina's still-fragile democracy was dealing with labor strikes, hyperinflation, and power shortages that meant walking up and down the sixteen flights to my apartment in semi-dark stairwells, lit by tea lights on the landings. A few weeks before I'd come to Argentina, a retired general had attempted a coup, and my mother had warned, "This will be your Vietnam." I thought she was a killjoy, her worry a yoke I had to break.

Army tanks rolled past my neighborhood café—past bistros, banks, currency exchanges, clothing boutiques, shoe shops, stationery stores—toward La Tablada military garrison, taken over by guerrillas. My roommate, Maria, and I watched from a table by the window, sipping *café con leche*.

Maria sighed. "I want to go home. I'm too old for this."

I'd met her when she stopped by the *Herald*, looking for work. She had written for the arts section of the *St. Petersburg Times*, but the *Herald* had a small staff and wasn't hiring anymore. I'd slipped in because someone had just left the paper when I showed up with a thick envelope of work: my articles for the foreign affairs journal, my thesis on the Latin American debt crisis, and my research paper on the 1973 oil embargo—written as a summer intern for a Washington DC think tank. "I'm not hiring any more foreigners," the editor had said. I left the envelope on his desk. He called that afternoon. "Can you start tomorrow?" I did. And later, when I'd run into experienced journalists who'd been turned away by the *Herald* like Maria, they'd always ask, "How did *you* get that job?"

Maria found work as an English teacher and freelance writer for the Associated Press, doing features like her piece on *la mufa*—the Argentine "blues." She'd come to Buenos Aires because she had family in Argentina, and she wanted to travel and write, like me. But she was seven years older than me, about to turn thirty, and she had grown weary of the violence, remembering how her brother swiftly left the country after the last military coup. She wanted to go back to the United States to find a job, meet a man, maybe have children. It seemed like a betrayal to the free spirit in me, since Maria had given me her well-worn copy of Simone de Beauvoir's autobiography. But the truth is that Argentina had become unmanageable for me, too. Hyperinflation had shrunk the value of my salary from a livable $300 a month to only $30 in less than a year. I couldn't even cover my half of the rent with that, and now that Maria was leaving, I'd have to pay the full $160 a month. The rent didn't fluctuate. My landlord set it in dollars.

I took a sip of my *café con leche*. "I want to travel before I go."

It was the end of summer in Argentina, the seasons reversing below the equator, when I bought an Aérolinas Argentinas ticket with unlimited stops for a month and left, seeing penguins in Tierra del Fuego, glaciers in Patagonia, the Bambi forest in Bariloche, the wine country in Mendoza, gauchos on horseback in Salta, sandhills striped rose, lime, and bone in Jujuy. I crossed the Andes to Chile, spending two nervous days in Santiago during Pinochet's military rule, and then took a plane to La Paz, where Bolivian women wore English bowler hats and baby-doll skirts. Now I was on my way to Machu Picchu, the Inca ruins in the Peruvian Andes.

It was dusk when the minivan pulled into Puno, a muddy border town on Titicaca's shore. I couldn't get over the mud. It covered most of the cobblestone roads, except for patches of bone-colored rock that poked through now and again. Chocolate-brown mud spread over everything, moist and thick as manure. A Peruvian man walked toward Dirk and me, stepping quickly through the mud without seeming to get stuck. The man's poncho bounced up and down with each of his steps. His cheekbones protruded high, and the cavity below sunk in deep. His skin resembled redwood, a blend of rust and mustard and brown that I'd seen in Bolivia, too. Argentina has so much European blood that sometimes you'd think you were in France or Italy or Spain instead. The man stared at Dirk and me.

"*Viajeros?*" He wondered if we were travelers.

"*Llegamos.*" I said the Spanish word for "arrived" the way I'd learned to in Argentina.

"*Argentina?*"

"*Sí.*"

My instincts told me it was better to lie. The United States didn't have the best reputation in Latin America because of the Central Intelligence Agency's history of backing coups, and the lie was easy to pull off with my accent and long chestnut hair, a typical Argentine look. So I let him think he'd guessed right, that I was an Argentine. A neighbor, backpacking in the Andes.

The man smiled, his cheekbones rising into his dark, deep-set eyes, as he bounded past us toward the docks. The silver surface of Lake Titicaca rippled at the end of that mud-caked road.

That night, after fish and fries, Dirk and I went to a pub. It looked English. Bronze beer taps and a mahogany bar. Backpackers in blue jeans and flannel shirts crowded the place.

Dirk held up his beer and sipped. "There was a woman in Brazil." He grinned, taking a puff of his cigarette. I could see the yellow tint of his teeth. "She wants me to stay."

"Why didn't you?"

Dirk laughed, a casual and carefree laugh that somehow told me he only wanted pleasure out of life. "I don't make my life in Brazil, but it is beautiful. Have you been?"

"Just Rio," I said.

"You don't go north to Bahía?"

"I don't think I'll get up that far." I shrugged.

He nodded and grinned as if listening to drums beat. "The beaches and the people, so beautiful."

"Someday," I said.

The door to the pub swung open. A man walked in, and I watched him, sucking in a deep breath, the way I do huffing up a big hill on a run. I held the air inside, as if letting it out would distract me from the backpacker. He smiled and stared as he sauntered toward me, lean and tall. *He's the one*, ran through my mind. I had never felt that kind of certainty. It was the way he looked at me—as if saying, *You bet I am*—as he headed to the back of the pub and up the stairs to the balcony. I turned and watched his plaid flannel shirt flop against the back pockets of his Levi's, hanging low on his hips.

Dirk and I walked to the train station the next morning. A ticket line overflowed into the street. Mostly men with wool ponchos and long black hair. I waited in line, and Dirk went on ahead. He asked a man up front to buy a ticket for him in exchange for a few pesos. Dirk came back with a ticket to Arequipa. He scribbled his address in my journal and kissed my cheek. I might have gone with him to the front of the line if we were going in the same direction. But he was heading south toward Chile, and I was moving north to Cusco and Machu Picchu. Besides, if the Peruvians had to wait, I'd wait, too.

"Why do you wait in such lines?" a baritone voice breathed into my ear.

I turned to see the backpacker from the pub.

"I need a ticket for Cusco," I said.

He smiled. "Come, I know a better way."

"Okay."

I followed him down the path, and we walked into a travel agency near the main road, a one-room office with a counter. Posters of Machu Picchu blown up on the walls. "*Necessitamos dos billetes a Cusco, por favor.*" He spoke Spanish well, like me.

"Where do you stay?" he asked.

"The hostel next to the pub." I pointed up the hill and waved right. "That side of the square."

"Tomorrow morning." He nodded his head. "Seven o'clock."

My backpack hung heavy on my shoulders as I trekked down the hostel stairwell in the morning. It smelled musky, like wet laundry gone sour. A yellow cab drove up as I reached the front stoop on the cobblestone square.

"Here, give me your bag." He opened the trunk and found room for my big blue backpack among the others. The trunk was stuffed full. "Come, get in," he said.

I got into the car already filled with travelers. He slid in next to me, closed the taxi door, and told the driver to get us to the train station in the neighboring town. Our train to Cusco departed from there.

"What's your name?" he asked, his nose nearly resting on my cheek.

"Karol."

"Aviv," he said, pronouncing his name Ah-*veev*. He looked like an American college student with his wire-rimmed glasses, shaggy chestnut hair, plaid flannel shirt, and faded Levi's.

Aviv looked at the backpacker beside me in the cab. "This is Uri." He had black curls and aquamarine eyes.

"Hi, Uri," I said.

He gave me a groggy morning hello.

Aviv then pointed at the women in the front seat. "This is Liat and Mihal." Their names sounded like Lee-*ot* and Mee-*hal* with a guttural *h*.

"You're American?" Aviv studied me now, like I'd studied him in the pub.

"Yes, and you?"

"We are Israeli, all of us in this car but you and the driver. We are traveling together for some days now. We meet in Bolivia, and we stay together after that."

I remembered the first Israeli I'd met on the road. I'd taken him for an American soldier at first. Big blue eyes, short-cropped, dusty blond hair and bodybuilder biceps. He sat next to me on the plane out of El Calafate, an Argentine village along the Andes, where the Perito Moreno Glacier spawned blue-and-white icebergs.

"I met an Israeli in Patagonia," I said.

"We're all traveling after our military service. We call it the tax for living in Israel," Aviv chuckled. "Men go in the army three years, the women two years, and then we go on a big trip. Some are going to South America, and some are going to the Far East. We are going away from the fighting, so much fighting. I am liking peace very much, peace like you have on a sheep farm. Okay, maybe not a sheep farm in Peru, where everything is looking so peaceful, but still you have terrorists coming to make problems. Peace like you have on a sheep farm in New Zealand."

2

Machu Picchu

The train looked like a diner. Brown vinyl benches tucked under beige Formica tabletops, all along the car on both sides. The Israelis found a booth near the entrance. No room for me. I scanned for an open seat, spotted one several rows back, and hustled for it. Aviv came over to strap my bag to the metal rack above.

"You have to tie the bags," he said. "A lot of things get stolen on the trains."

"Thanks."

Aviv went back to his seat.

A Peruvian man peeled oranges for his little boy and girl. I tried not to stare at the oranges. I hadn't had any breakfast and didn't have anything on me. One of the children offered me a slice. I looked at the father before accepting it. He smiled, and I slid the slice into my mouth.

With a jerk, the train rolled out of the station. I gazed out of the window at flocks of sheep roaming green hills under a gray sky.

"Do you want to play cards?" Aviv asked, sitting down on the corner of the table in front of me.

"Sure."

"I'll teach you a game we play in the army." He took out a pack of cards and a bag of peanuts. I grabbed a handful.

As he flipped cards to demonstrate the game of Whist, I could not concentrate on his words. All I noticed were his hands. His fingers were as lean as the rest of him. His knuckles protruded, like burls on a maple. The skin was bronzed and cracked around the cuticles, like a working-man's. I liked his hands.

"Have you got it?"

"I think so. Let's try a game."

I soon caught on.

"Where do you live in Israel?"

"A small town, the north," he said. "Are you from New York?"

"Not far. Connecticut. Very boring."

"Boring sounds good." He beamed. "Do you have paper?"

"Sure." I pulled out my journal and flipped to a blank page.

"I will draw a map." He made a quick sketch of his country. "You see, there is Jerusalem, Tel Aviv, and Haifa. I'm in Kiryat Bialik, right here." He pointed to a dot just above the northern port of Haifa.

"You've been traveling long?" I asked.

"I've been six months traveling. Argentina, Chile, Brazil, Bolivia, Peru," Aviv said, counting countries with his fingers. "How long you have been in South America?"

"About a year."

"You travel one year?"

"No, I spent most of that time working for a newspaper in Buenos Aires."

He tapped my journal. "You are the journalist, and I am the traveler."

"I keep a journal because I don't like to forget what I've seen," I said.

"Why do you go to Argentina?"

"I'd have traveled the world if I'd had the money, but I didn't, and my mother said I had to get a job. So I stayed with an Argentine friend from school and got a job."

"Tell me, have you been to Torres del Paine in the south of Chile?"

"No, just Santiago."

"Torres del Paine is such a beautiful place. I was hiking in the mountains there. I want to go again." He smiled.

"I only went to the south of Argentina. I loved Calafate, the glaciers and icebergs. They were so blue," I said, biting my lower lip. "Did you go?"

"Yes, I was there, and Bariloche, too."

"I didn't like Bariloche, except for the hot cocoa served with a stick of flaky chocolate that looked like a tree branch."

"I know this drink," Aviv said. "But why you don't like Bariloche?"

"It was so touristy."

Aviv stopped to consider my criticism for a moment, then continued. "I've liked it very much. We don't have such mountains and forests in Israel."

"You went to Rio?"

"Yes, for Carnival. But the best of Brazil is the north."

"I've heard."

"You didn't go?"

"Next time I'd go to the north of Brazil, Colombia, Ecuador, Venezuela."

"Me, too."

I made a wish, the kind I'd made blowing out candles on a cake as a girl, that Aviv and I could someday tour those countries together. Aviv was the first traveler who made me feel this way. I liked traveling alone, always taking my time to explore and observe and think, always meeting someone along the way, but everyone else, including Dirk, eventually seemed like an intrusion on my solitude, even if slight. Aviv was the only one who made me feel as free as I had been going alone. I felt a rush and put my hand on his.

"So, how do you know Spanish so well?"

"My family, we lived in Mexico."

"When?"

"I was very young. My Spanish, it was very bad. I didn't speak for something like six months. Then one day I start to speak, and I don't shut up for nothing." He laughed.

"The same thing happened to me. I'd had some classes in college and lived with some Argentine students for a while, but forget it, nothing would come out of my mouth. I'd sit silently at dinner and try to understand until I got too tired to listen anymore. Then all of a sudden, I don't know why, words came out of my mouth. I was chatting up the ice cream man, the grocery store clerk, my doorman."

Aviv grinned. "So why do you leave?"

"Hyperinflation. I couldn't live off my salary anymore."

Aviv nodded, a knowing nod, one that told me he knew what was going on in places like Argentina. Places where things got messy. Places like his homeland.

"You go home now?"

"Yes, after Machu Picchu."

"Have you gone to Taquile?"

"The reed islands on Lake Titicaca?"

"No, not the reed islands. A real island on Lake Titicaca.

The people, they are so beautiful. I make a sign to help them with their fight."

"Their fight?"

"The island people, they don't want boats from Puno taking tourists to the island. They only want their own boats to take all the tourists. The people, they don't have any other way to make money. They need the money to buy coffee and sugar, all the things they don't have on the island. They share the money. It's for all the people. I make a sign with the other Israelis, Uri and Mihal and Liat. The people, they are so happy we make this sign. We play soccer to celebrate."

I'd had friends from Penn who protested apartheid, joining a sit-in to pressure the university to divest from South Africa, but I always wondered who they would become after school, when we no longer lived in the protective bubble of a liberal arts college. But Aviv seemed like someone who'd never sell out, who'd never lose his idealism, who'd never let go of his dreams.

"I'll go on my way back to Buenos Aires." I wanted to see the island and his sign.

We played cards and talked for hours, about everything—our travels, Argentina, the army, the apples he had picked to finance his trip. When he returned to his seat, I heard laughter and guessed his friends were ribbing him about his interest in the American. Me.

I felt a rumble and woke to nightfall. The train pulled into the station in Cusco. Aviv was already untying my backpack.

"You slept," he said, smiling.

"We're here already?"

It was night, but I could see that Cusco looked medieval. Cobblestone roads, stone facades, shingled roofs peaking in triangles, one after another. Aviv hailed a cab and directed the driver to a hostel he'd read about in his guide. The car bumped up the jagged stone path and left us at the hostel. It looked like a fortress, the kind that protected Scottish kings.

· Aviv nudged me in the morning. He already had on his jeans and flannel shirt. "We go for breakfast."

"Oh, okay, what time is it?"

"It's almost nine o'clock. Usually, we're going out much earlier."

"We go now," Mihal said.

"We go later," Aviv said, looking at me.

Uri followed Liat and Mihal out of the room.

I went into the bathroom to change, and when I came out, Aviv was sitting on one of the single beds studying the *South American Traveler's Handbook*, the bible of serious backpackers. I had a guide that offered lengthy anthropological insights along with the practical things, which I mostly skipped over, preferring word-of-mouth tips from South Americans and travelers like Aviv.

"I know a place to eat. I hear about it from other travelers."

"You know everything. Me, I hardly know anything before I get where I'm going."

"I like to research everything. Come, let's go."

I wanted him to reach out, take my hands, wrap me around him, and kiss me. But he didn't. I walked out of the room behind him, watching his Levi's pockets and the rim of his flannel shirt. Outside, he walked next to me, keeping a friendly distance, the kind I'd kept with Dirk. We stepped over cobblestones that bumped along the road. Peruvians in ponchos dipped in and out among the stones, scaling hills and descending them without effort. But backpackers crept over the rock road, as if climbing a mountain ravine.

Aviv pointed to a fortress like our hostel. "This is where we eat. I have met a traveler in La Paz who said I must go here."

I followed Aviv up the stairs to the restaurant. Exposed beams crisscrossed above oak booths along the wall. "Here." He pointed to a booth across from the bar. We slid in.

"It looks like a pub," I said.

"It's a vegetarian place."

A waiter came over to us. "Do you want the muesli?"

"What's that?"

"Yogurt, fruit, granola, and honey."

"Okay, I never tried it."

Aviv asked the waiter for two mueslis.

"You never tried muesli?"

"No, I'm not a vegetarian, not by a long stretch. My parents are from Nebraska, and everybody from Nebraska eats meat."

"I don't like how it looks before it is cooked, so I tell my mother I'm not eating meat anymore. I am only twelve when I tell her this, and since then I don't eat meat."

"I'd never get away with that. My mother was tough."

I used to argue with my mother mostly about clothes and hair. The faded, ripped jeans I'd wear or the split ends on my long swimmer's hair I'd refuse to cut. She once sent me to my father's barber to get the ends trimmed, and I ended up with a Dorothy Hamill. "That's not fair," I'd say. "I don't care if it's fair. I'm your mother, and I make the rules," she'd say. I tried to run away once but only made it to the hemlocks in the front yard.

"I tell you a story. When I am a little boy and we live in Mexico, my mother and father take me to the United States for a vacation. We drive through the Mojave Desert, and I want grapes. I tell my mother, 'Ima'—that is the Hebrew word for 'mother'—'Ima, I want grapes.' So my mother says to me, 'Aviv, we are in the desert, we can't find grapes here. You have to wait.' And I say to her, 'No, Ima, I want grapes.' So she finds me strawberries, and I say, 'No, Ima, I want grapes.' Then she says to me, 'But Aviv, we are lucky to find strawberries in the desert. We can't find the grapes. You have to wait.' But I tell her again, 'No, Ima, I want grapes.' I don't eat the strawberries. My father keeps driving. Then my mother finds another place, and she comes to me with grapes."

The waiter set down gray ceramic bowls full of yogurt, granola, cantaloupe, blueberries, strawberries, and red-wine grapes. I tried a spoonful.

"This is really good. Still, I don't think I'll become a vegetarian."

"This is what I'm eating, besides cottage cheese, rice, eggs, and fish. Sandwiches of avocados, tomatoes, and olives on a pita. And apples. Apples every day. Apples are the best for me. I am eating them always. Sometimes I am buying a big bag of apples and eating them all in one day. Maybe one dozen, even more. When I'm picking apples to save money for this trip, I am picking one and eating one, picking one and eating one."

"I like peanut butter best. I used to eat it right out of the jar."

Aviv spooned some yogurt, grapes, and honey into his mouth.

"Peanut butter is okay. But not like apples. Nothing is like apples, for me."

Aviv and I sat in a chapel, quietly looking at the golden trunk by the pulpit and the stained glass windows that wrapped around the chapel, full of Bible stories I'd learned in Sunday school. We'd been together for several days, since he pulled me out of the train line in Puno, but this was our first day alone, and I had decided if he didn't kiss me soon, I was going to move on. Then I felt his lips on mine, our first kiss, inside that tiny chapel, a warm spring flowing inside of me. We left the chapel, holding hands.

Cusco had seemed medieval and gray until then. Now I noticed the Gothic church spire pointing toward the baby-blue sky and evergreen Andes peeking over stone forts, guarding the cobblestone square. A Peruvian woman leaned against a column with her loom. She stretched one leg out on the stone path and tucked the other one under her navy skirt. She flipped back her long black braid as she pulled threads with her butternut hands. She jerked the threads into place, one after another. Threads of rose and violet and blue, weaving them into diamonds on a belt. She had already made half of the belt, the kind children carried in bundles as they worked the cobblestone plaza in bare feet.

Aviv and I sat down on a wooden bench in the center of the square. Children pranced over the cool stones toward us and made a semicircle around us. They stretched out their suntanned arms, clutching handmade belts and ceramic jars painted with falcons and warriors.

"Where are you from?" asked the tallest, a girl.

"I'm American, and he's Israeli."

"Jerusalem, the capital of Israel. Paris, the capital of France. Mitterand, the president of France," she said.

"How did you learn English and all of those facts? Amazing," I said.

"From the tourists," she said, sounding so matter-of-fact. "My name is Betty. I need shoes and a notebook for school."

The other children grabbed onto her skirt hem and elbows and shoulders, waiting to see what we would do. Would we buy her a pair of shoes and a notebook for school? They looked up at Betty, scanning her black ponytail and ebony stare, and then they looked back at us, mouths agape, waiting to see what would happen.

"You don't have a notebook for school?" I asked. They all looked at Betty again.

"No. I need a notebook—and shoes," she said, pointing to her black cotton Mary Janes. She wore no socks, and her chopstick legs seemed almost green from the cold. It was early April, and the Andean foothills were cool.

"Here," Aviv said. He handed her a few bills. "I'll take a jar."

Betty snatched the cash and plunked a jar into his palm and dashed off over the cobblestones to the other side of the courtyard, her entourage following, a goose and her gaggle.

Aviv and I sat on the roadside waiting for the bus to Machu Picchu. A dirt path cut through the green foothills, so green they looked like a fertilized lawn. We squatted outside a restaurant shack. Weathered gray like Cape Cod homes I'd seen on family vacations as a child. Sun and rain beat hard on the wood, bleaching it from brown to driftwood gray. Buttercups dimpled the valley across the road, the hillside sloping down into a valley that stretched out flat like a Nebraska cornfield. Beyond the valley, green mountains rolled up and up and up, forming an Andean ridge that ran as far as I could see along the horizon.

Inside the shack, a woman with molasses skin and black-bean eyes leaned into the counter.

"When does the bus come?" Aviv asked in Spanish.

Her raven hair, pulled back off her face, hung in a braid down her back.

"Look, don't know, could be hours," she told us.

"Sit, sit." She pointed toward a picnic table near the doorway. We could watch for the bus from inside, she said. We ordered potato and leek soup, the only item on the menu, spelled out in Spanish on a blackboard behind the counter.

An hour later, the bus had not come. We walked out to the roadside again and crouched.

"Hey, there's a car." I pointed down the road. "Let's go for it. We'll never get out of here unless we hitch a ride."

We waved our hands as if making snow angels and tried to catch the attention of the silver car driving toward us along the hillside road. A cloud of dirt kicked up in our faces. The car screeched to a stop just ahead of us, and we trotted for it. The driver rolled down his window. He wore slacks, a button-down shirt, and penny loafers. His black hair was cropped short like a fifties preppy.

"Going to Machu Picchu," Aviv said in Spanish.

"Get in," the driver said.

The driver sped up around the bend, along the edge of the green slopes that dipped down into the valley. Aviv nudged me in the shoulder and pointed to the gun under the driver's side seat. My grandfather, a Nebraska rancher on the sheriff's posse, used to carry a loaded pistol under his car seat for protection from people like Charlie Starkweather, who'd gone on a killing spree. Peru had a different kind of violence. Shining Path guerrillas were kidnapping, torturing, and killing Peruvians and some foreigners. The car jerked to a stop. A mound of red-brown dirt blocked our path.

"Workers are protesting," the driver said. He darted a glance down the valley and back to the dirt blockade. "I have a gun for such problems," he said. He had the menacing look of a paramilitary man.

"We can't pass?" Aviv asked.

"No," the driver said. "But if you walk down there, down into the farms, you can pass to another village, and there you can find a bus."

Aviv led the way into the valley and through a cornfield. Corn silk puffing out of pale green husks brushed my shoulders. On the other side of the field, we found a paved road. It looked like it would take us to Machu Picchu, if we walked and walked and walked.

"We can't walk all the way," Aviv said. "This is too much walking."

I pointed. "There, that's our ride. Come on."

Aviv and I hailed a truck. The driver stopped and told us to climb up. I grabbed the ladder on the side of the truck and scaled up to a bed of dusty brown potatoes heaped a story high. I crawled on top of the potatoes and clutched onto the wood railing that hemmed in the potatoes.

"Sort of like a hayride," I said.

Aviv laughed.

The truck bumped along the road, potatoes popping up and down, though none flipped out of the truck. I gripped onto the railing the way I held onto the safety bars of a roller coaster.

The potato truck pulled into a cobblestone courtyard at dusk. When we climbed down, the driver pointed to the train tracks. "There, that is where you will find the train to Machu Picchu, but it won't leave until the morning."

"Come, this way," Aviv said. He pointed to a hostel next to the train station.

Aviv lay on the bed, one leg on the wide-plank pine floor and the other stretched along the mattress, his Levi's coated in potato dust. His flannel shirt flipped up over his stomach. His skin was honey-colored from the Brazilian sun. He stared at me with easy eyes, smiling. I pulled the curtains off their hooks and went to him.

In the morning, we took a train to Machu Picchu. The Inca ruins were nestled on an Andean ridge. The mountains were green, a muted green, unlike the bright lime of the foothills below. A gray river snaked through the valley. A staircase scaled a jutting peak. Llamas bobbed their swan-like necks and bleated as they pranced about the ruins. A Peruvian man in a red poncho whistled folk tunes into his reed flute.

"Look, over there," Aviv pointed to a stone slab at the

far edge of the ruins. "That is where they are sacrificing virgins to their gods."

Aviv and I walked over to the block, big and rectangular like a coffin. I studied the granite slab, searching the worn surface, as if I might see some lingering evidence of blood.

"Do you think it's true?"

"Of course," Aviv said. "People do anything in the name of God."

3

Schlepper

Back at home in Connecticut, I sat at the kitchen table with my mother, looking out the picture window while she read my article. It was May, and the white dogwood and the hot-pink azaleas were in bloom.

"Why don't you start here," she said.

"With the cartoon?" I said.

Somewhere in the middle of the story, I'd described a Buenos Aires newspaper sketch that lampooned how cool Argentines stay during national crises—still packing their bags for the beach, even though the country seemed poised for another coup before the first presidential transition since the military left power.

"It's a whole lot catchier." She still had a midwestern twang, after nearly twenty years in Connecticut.

"Nobody will get it," I said.

"Sure they will. Why don't you start like this: The scene is a beach."

I scribbled lines onto paper. "How about this? The scene

is a beach with an Argentine couple basking in the sun, sipping drinks. One says casually to the other, 'How close we came to losing democracy.'"

"That's the way to start, something catchy, hook people in," she said.

The telephone rang. My mother reached for the phone.

"It's Aviv." She raised her eyebrows as she handed me the phone. I had not told her about him.

"Aviv?"

"That's me."

"Where are you?"

"Brooklyn."

"Brooklyn?"

"I stay one week with friends of my parents. Then I say, why don't I find work and stay. So now I'm with Schleppers. They're Israeli. They give me work as a mover. My tired muscles will be happy to tell you all about it." He chuckled.

"I'm moving to the city soon," I said.

"When?"

"When I find an apartment."

"I think you should live with me."

"I couldn't do that. What would I do when you leave?"

"You would miss me?"

"Yes."

"Can I see you?"

"Soon."

"You promise?"

"I promise."

"Now I have to go. Do you remember Rosanna, the woman I met in Brazil. She is here working as a nanny. We go to the movies now," Aviv said.

"Oh, yes, okay," I said.

He'd met Rosanna in the north of Brazil, before he met me. Now she was in New York? How could he ask me to live with him and then run off to see Rosanna?

After I got off the phone, my mother asked, "Who's Aviv?"

"I met him in Peru," I said.

"You didn't mention him."

"I didn't think I'd ever see him again, but he's here, and he wants to live with me. Then he says he's got to go, he's meeting Rosanna."

"Who's Rosanna?"

"Some woman he met in Brazil."

"Well is he worth getting so upset over?"

"I don't know. Yes, yes, he is."

Aviv and I explored Inca ruins in the Peruvian Andes for two weeks before taking the train back to Puno, the Bolivian border town on Lake Titicaca. I stopped there and took a boat to the reed islands and then Taquile. As my boat approached, islanders hurried down the steep steps of the moon shaped island, hurling stones at nearby boats coming from the mainland. I could see Aviv's protest sign, still on the docks. Aviv had gone ahead to Bolivia, and I met up with him in La Paz.

It was crisp in the Altiplano as Aviv and I hiked up and down the streets of La Paz, steep as San Francisco's. Bolivian men in colorful stocking caps and women in English bowler hats and baby-doll skirts crowded the streets, selling supplies like batteries, razors, and aftershave along with alpaca sweaters, coca tea leaves, and dried llama fetuses, cradled in small baskets as fertility amulets. I bought a stocking cap, knit in bands of electric pinks, blues, yellows, and greens that I hung on my wall after I moved to New York, and Aviv bought a fleece coat that he wrapped around me as we waited for my bus to Buenos Aires.

I had to go back to Argentina and pack a year-and-a-half's worth of belongings into my backpack and suitcases and cardboard boxes before flying home, while Aviv had a ticket from La Paz to San Francisco to see Dov, his father's son from his first marriage to a woman who lived on a kibbutz near the Golan Heights. Dov planned to return to the kibbutz with his wife and daughters once he finished his PhD. Aviv's eyes began to tear up, the way mine did after my bus began to pull away.

The city felt like a sauna and smelled of garbage, piled up on the sidewalks because of the sanitation strike, as I went for a run along Central Park, carefully avoiding the inside of the park, where a jogger had been raped and bashed in the head by teenagers only weeks before I moved to the city that summer. The unidentified woman would become famously known as the "Central Park jogger," and my street smarts kept me out of the park until it had become a much, much tamer place.

As I ran along Central Park South, I noticed Aviv ahead of me, walking toward the Salute to Israel Parade on Fifth Avenue. I'd been in the city for several weeks, sharing a small place near the park with Jeanne, a friend from college who introduced me to Gabriel García Márquez's *One Hundred Years of Solitude*, inspiring my passion for Latin American literature: Isabel Allende's *The Stories of Eva Luna*,

Jorge Amado's *Doña Flor and Her Two Husbands*, Jorge Luis Borges's *Labyrinths*, Julio Cortázar's *Hopscotch*, Carlos Fuentes's *The Old Gringo*, Mario Vargas Llosa's *The Real Life of Alejandro Mayta*, and much, much later Guillermo Rosales's *The Halfway House*, Roberto Bolaño's *2666*—authors from Argentina, Brazil, Chile, Colombia, Cuba, Mexico, Peru.

I hadn't called Aviv, like I'd promised. I worried some about Rosanna, though Aviv spoke about her casually, like a friend instead of a lover. She was almost ten years older than Aviv, and he said she was "sometimes beautiful, sometimes not, like Sônia Braga," the sensual Brazilian actress in *Kiss of the Spiderwoman*. Only a tough critic like Aviv would see her that way, so I knew that Rosanna was probably a striking brunette, too, but the truth is the thought of Aviv leaving worried me more.

I called anyway, and we met at a diner that night.

"I saw you today, near the park."

"You should have come to me."

"I was going jogging, and I don't know, I felt nervous."

"Nervous, but why?"

"To see you in New York. Maybe it would be different."

"But there is no difference for me."

"I'm glad." I paused. "But what about Rosanna?"

"Rosanna, she's working as a nanny."

"I know she's working as a nanny, but what about her?"

"I understand you. We are just friends. That is all."

"Just friends? But you went to the movies together."

"Rosanna is only a friend, nothing more."

I still felt raw about it, but I let it go. "So, you had no trouble finding a place to live?"

"No trouble. I took the first place I've seen. You should see the floor. It's painted the color of a mango. And there are plants everywhere."

"So have you seen much of New York?"

"I've been working all over. The Village, Brooklyn, Queens, New Jersey. New Jersey looks like such a nice place. I tell myself I would like to live in a place like New Jersey."

"New Jersey? That's boring. Manhattan is so much better."

"It has so much energy, I can't sleep. I always feel I am missing something."

"That's what I like, knowing there's always something new, and if you miss it today, something else will come along."

Aviv sighed. "Maybe if I knew I could live here always, I would feel different. But I'm only here for a few months."

"When will you go?"

"Maybe September. I have only done the army. Now I must go and study at the university."

"What will you study?"

"Computers at the Technion. You have this school, MIT— they say in Israel that the Technion is like this school."

"It must be the best."

"It's the best."

"I'm starting to think about graduate school."

"What do you study?"

"Latin America, maybe get a job with a big newspaper so I can earn a living."

Aviv smiled. "I can help you become an Israeli expert."

We began to see each other almost every night after work, spending the entire weekend together, exploring the city's contours when it was still an intensely bohemian and dangerous place, going to diners for simple meals—scrambled eggs and home fries, soup and grilled cheese sandwiches—and small cafés for cappuccino and cheesecake and long soulful talks, following live music or a movie, usually independent or foreign. Aviv's favorite was *Betty Blue*, a French film about a passionate, but tortured, romance between an aspiring writer who works as a handyman and his obsessive girlfriend that begins with a long scene of lovemaking.

I'd gone to the Christian Science Sunday school, like my mother and her mother—the daughter of a Nebraska dentist who read Mary Baker Eddy's textbook, *Science and Health with Key to the Scriptures*, and adopted the religion that relied on healing through prayer and forbid drinking, smoking, or sex outside of marriage. Alcohol, cigarettes, and drugs didn't interest me, but abstention was an impossible standard for a young woman who studied the world map on her shower curtain instead of wedding magazines.

Aviv's taste in films seemed radically defiant and sophisticated. He was a scathing critic of "typical American movies"—a category that seemed to cover almost anything that wasn't made by Woody Allen or Spike Lee. Our first argument was over *Dead Poet's Society*. It didn't matter that the film was directed by Peter Weir, an Australian; it was still a "typical American movie." Aviv was irritated by the fragile young man in the film, an aspiring actor who commits suicide after his father crushes his dreams by transferring him from an American prep school, where he's inspired by theater, poetry, and his brilliant teacher who urges his students to carpe diem—"seize the day"— to the stale future of a military academy. "I don't want to see this guy in Israel," Aviv said.

I understood Aviv, the idealist who'd had no choice but to serve in the military, like every other Israeli boy and girl. It didn't matter that he'd served in a noncombat role, working with computers instead of guns, during his mandatory military service. He'd lost precious years in the army when typical Americans were in college, like me. But I understood the sensitive boy in the film, too. After my first year of college, inspired by my Shakespeare professor on loan from Princeton, I told my mother that I wanted to study English and become a writer. My mother shot back with her usual fierceness—the cowgirl confidence of a cattle rancher's daughter that I feared until I was old enough to admire it—"I won't have you lollygag around reading books, you hear me, Karol Lynn."

It was an especially egregious plan because of the twenty-five thousand dollars my father was spending on tuition, room, and board to send me to Penn. My mother wanted me to study something professional, something that would help me get a job when I graduated. "A woman needs to be able to support herself in this world. Besides, if you want to become a writer you have to have something to write about." I'd never won an argument with my mother, hard as I'd tried—always getting into trouble over my lip, too much lip—but for the first time I didn't fight her.

And to be fair, this news was probably coming as a surprise to my mother, and in some ways to me, too, having shown my creativity through painting and drawing until now, even winning a citywide prize for a piece in the eighth grade, though it was always a slightly dubious award to me because I'd copied the image of the sphinx, the way I copied faces in fashion magazines, not knowing that my teacher would submit it for competition. But when it came to books and writing, something I considered to be the domain of Ivy League intellectuals, and while, technically, I would become one of them, I had come from the down-to-earth pioneers of Nebraska and Iowa and Wyoming. Farmers, ranchers, blacksmiths, dentists, pilots, soldiers, engineers, small-business owners, a railroad clerk, a coal-car worker, a secretary, and a dancer. My mother's mother, Lulalee, toured the country with the Chester Hale Girls and then joined the Radio City Rockettes before marrying my grandfather, the hump pilot. He first saw her in a photograph on his sister's piano. "I'm going to marry that woman," he said to his sister. She had married my grandmother's brother—a bomber pilot who'd get shot down and killed in action on a mission to Münster, Germany, during World War II, winning a posthumous Purple Heart. My grandfather, a voracious speed reader who disdained the eastern establishment, would write a fantastical short story collection called "The Purple World." It was never published.

While I had the drive to tell stories, I had no proof of its possibility as a profession and couldn't match my mother's conviction about the best way to proceed, couldn't come to the defense of my plan when it still seemed too uncertain and far off, so I sheepishly got off the phone, settling on international relations, so I could write about other countries, and economics, to convince my mother I'd find a job, while slowly sinking into a foggy malaise that lasted through college, lifting sometime in South America, where I'd wake up in the mornings after my 3 p.m.–through–midnight shift at the newspaper and write. Every day.

4
Revital

Aviv sat next to me on the couch of his roomy, two-bedroom apartment in Harlem that he shared with a Californian. He'd painted the floor mango, like Aviv had said, and filled the place with plants. It had a relaxed, tropical feel that suited Aviv. He had just finished a pickup basketball game on the West 104th Street court, a few blocks away.

"You know, I wanted to be in the NBA," Aviv said.

"A basketball star?"

"Too late for such dreams."

"Never too late."

Aviv shook his head.

"My sister Revital, she is coming to New York. She wants to see the Amish."

"I went with my family as a girl. We stayed on a Mennonite farm and milked the cows."

"My sister, she likes traveling, too. After she finishes with the army, she travels in South America like me. Then she studies dance in New York before she goes home to Israel."

"When did she live here?"

"Something like ten years ago."

"She's ten years older?"

"Almost. My other sister, Ofra, she's like eight years more than me. My brother, Dov, he's forty."

"Forty! That's almost as old as my parents."

"My mother is more than sixty, and my father, he's almost seventy."

"Seventy. One of my grandmothers is about that."

Aviv looked away, telling me later how this embarrassed him as a boy. Sarah was forty, and Moshe almost fifty, when Aviv was born—the youngest by far of his father's four children. When Aviv was growing up, Moshe was too old to serve in the military like Aviv's friends' fathers did, and this made Aviv so ashamed that he ignored Moshe on a school field trip, pretending that he wasn't his father.

My father was also the youngest child of older parents, but he and my mother married young and had their three children by the time my mother was thirty. My sister, Cindy, was the baby, like my father and Aviv. She was only six years younger, but she was finishing elementary school by the time I left for college, and once I left, I hardly came home except for Thanksgiving, Christmas, and summer breaks. I was the rebellious and hypersensitive middle child, and my year-and-a-half-older brother, Mike, was so vigorously competitive with me that only he could open the door to our house, only he could own the hallways of our high school, only he could choose a TV show or radio station—always cartoons and kung fu movies, jazz and blues. My mother said that when I was a baby, she caught him clutching my foot, slowly advancing and retreating as if wanting to twist it off and forcing himself back.

"Revital, she works as a waitress while she studies. She works so hard, my sister."

"Does she perform?"

"Not so much since the cancer."

"Is she okay?"

"She is okay, except they took everything out. She can't have children."

"When did this happen?"

"Something like two years ago. For me, it was the last six months of the army. I move to a base in Tel Aviv, where she lives. I have a special arrangement so I can take care of my sister. She was so sick. All her hair fell out, everywhere, not just from her head. She used to have hair just like yours, even longer, like this." He pointed to his waist.

"What about your parents?"

"Revital says my mother makes her nervous." Aviv had told me that his mother had been hit by a car while he was in high school, injuring her head so badly that she lost consciousness. When she woke in the hospital, she spoke in her childhood language of Romanian before regaining her memory of Hebrew. Aviv said that his mother was never the same after the accident, compulsively cleaning and doing laundry.

"Nobody helped you?"

"Sometimes my sister Ofra was helping, but she has just been married so she doesn't have so much time, and sometimes Revital's boyfriend was helping, but mostly it was me."

"That must have been really hard."

"Something like that."

I'd never had to take care of anyone besides myself, and I admired Aviv for taking care of his sister. But I thought, What a burden for someone so young.

Revital pulled up to my apartment in a silver Nissan and opened the passenger door.

"Get in, guys," she said.

I liked her raspy voice.

"Do you mind if I smoke?" she asked, already fishing through her bag for cigarettes.

"I don't mind."

"You have a very nice girlfriend, Aviv."

Revital smiled and went on without any formal introduction as Yossi, her longtime boyfriend, drove us to see Amish farms in Lancaster, Pennsylvania. Revital had thick, short-cropped hair, almost ebony, like her almond-shaped eyes. Her name means "dewdrop" in Hebrew, and she was fine boned and petite like I'd imagined, but she didn't seem delicate at all; she seemed feisty and strong. I liked her already.

"You know, Karol, in Israel we have farms something like the Amish. We call this kind of farm a kibbutz—to live and to eat is free for everyone who's working on the kibbutz."

"One of my college roommates worked on a kibbutz."

"Very good, so maybe you will come to Israel."

"I'd like that."

Aviv smiled and squeezed my knee.

"So, Aviv, do you think you will travel more before you come home?"

"I want to go Mexico. Maybe Karol will come."

"I can't take time off yet. I just started my job. Besides, I only get two weeks."

"When can you take this time?"

"Fall," I said.

"Then we go in two months."

It was drizzling when we pulled up to an Amish farm on the wide-open plains of Pennsylvania Dutch country. "Go in there," Revital said, pointing to the farmhouse. A woman wearing a bonnet, apron, and long simple dress peered at us through the window as we drove down the private driveway toward the farmhouse. "Look," Revital said, pointing to a young Amish man, sitting erect in his horse-drawn carriage as it moved down the road. Yossi backed out of the driveway, and Revital snapped photos as we drove by.

5
Mexican Pyramids

A Mariachi musician strummed a *vihuela*, serenading Aviv and me as we studied the menu of the restaurant in Mexico City. It was October, and like I'd promised, I traveled with Aviv. He ordered black beans and corn tortillas with goat cheese. He held up a tiny bottle of lime-green salsa.

"Salsa *verde*, hot pepper sauce. We use it for the tortillas," Aviv said.

"I trust you."

The goat cheese smelled sweet, not like the pungent aroma I'd expected. Aviv doused the tortillas with salsa *verde*.

"This comes home with me to Israel," Aviv said.

The mealy tortilla, sweet cheese, and pungent salsa mingled in my mouth. "Spicy!"

"You like it?"

I nodded. "Spicy but good."

I did like it, even though my ear canals burned the way they did as a girl, when I'd eat my mother's tamale pie. After Aviv introduced me to Mexican hot sauce, I developed an enduring taste for spicy foods, and they curiously no longer inflamed my ears.

Aviv stood with his arms crossed over his chest, staring up at the balcony of the small building where he'd lived with his family as a boy. His mother had gone to Chile before coming to Israel, and she'd always wanted to go back to Latin America; so Moshe found a job teaching at a Hebrew school in Mexico City. The family stayed for two years, though they went without Revital, who had already graduated from high school and left home to travel in South America and go to college in New York before doing her mandatory two years in the Israeli military.

"Israel is a pressure cooker," Aviv said. "Sometimes I think I will live in Mexico."

"Do you think there will ever be peace?" I said.

"How do you make peace with people who hate you?"

"What about Egypt?"

"This is cold peace, not real peace. Come, we go see the pyramids."

We sat on the stone steps at the top of the Pyramid of the Sun, the largest of the pyramids among the Aztec ruins outside Mexico City. A dusty mall stretched out in front of us, like an abandoned football field. The bone-colored stone ruins faded into the whitish-blue sky.

"They make this for the gods," Aviv said.

"It's beautiful."

"This place where we sit, this is where they make sacrifices to the god of the sun."

I felt the surface of the stone, warm from the piercing sunlight. "Blood sacrifice?"

"The heart of a man."

"I'm dying of thirst. It's so dry."

Aviv reached into his backpack and pulled out a bottle of water. I took a big drink and shared the rest with Aviv. "We need water," he said, taking my hand. "We go now."

Children played in the central plaza as older men and women sold knit crafts and jewelry by the cathedral. Mexico reminded me of Peru. Old, stone, gothic. We'd walked through the main square many times that week, but this was my last day. I'd return to New York in the morning, and Aviv would continue to travel through Mexico and Guatemala before heading home. I wanted to urge him to stay in New York, to go to college and live with me. But I wanted it to be his choice, and so far he'd said he planned to go back to study computer science at the Technion in Haifa. He still had to take the entrance exams, having skipped them in the weeks while his mother was in a coma after her car accident, and besides he didn't want to work hard like his sister, who'd supported herself as a waitress while earning her bachelor's degree from Hunter College.

I thought about following him to Israel, but I didn't want to quit my job. It was a good job, a writing job, a paid gig covering Latin American conferences, and it was the first position that allowed me to live independently. I had enough money for rent and movies and even a trip to Mexico. And by now, I planned to apply to graduate school in Latin American studies, to learn more about the region and continue writing about it. I needed a reference from my boss, the vice president of the Americas Society. She was an author with a PhD in political science, an expert on Latin America. I couldn't afford to quit. Not yet.

6
Long Distance

I set down the newspaper and stared at Aviv's bicycle. It was the one he'd pedaled downtown to the Israeli moving companies he worked for that summer. The jobs had paid him enough to support himself in New York City, but he didn't like the work conditions. He'd come home exhausted and wounded from hauling furniture up and down four or five flights of stairs during the hot summer months. That might not have been as bad if the tips had compensated him fairly. But that usually didn't happen because the managers would quote prices without including the cost of packaging, so the movers like Aviv usually caught grief over the wide distance between the estimate and the final bill, and many of the customers didn't tip the movers, who were not to blame. More than that, Aviv disliked working with Israelis who lived underground lives without green cards, sometimes for years. They'd come to New York and other parts of the United States to make money. Once they'd made enough, they'd go home, but sometimes they never did. Aviv didn't want that kind of life. I didn't blame him, but still I didn't want him to go, and that bicycle was always there, reminding me that he was leaving.

The telephone rang, and I nicked my shin on the bike as I reached for the phone.

I heard a faint voice on the other end of the line saying, "It's me."

"Aviv?"

"I miss you."

"I miss you, too. Where are you?"

"Guatemala." He spoke softly and seemed down, very down.

"You sound so sad. What's happened?"

"The bus roll over."

"An accident?"

"Yes, an accident. The bus goes on its side. Some of the people are hurt. I think I break my arm."

"You broke your arm?"

"No. The doctor said no, this is not a break. But it was hurting so much."

"Did it stop hurting?"

"Yes. It stopped."

"Will you continue traveling?"

"No. I want to come back. I miss you."

Max Roach performed at the Blue Note with the Uptown String Quartet, led by his daughter Maxine. Their jazz was crisp, almost classical.

"Who's your favorite?" I asked.

"You." Aviv smiled.

I squeezed his knee. "I mean your favorite jazz artist."

"I like all the old guys, Oscar Peterson, Cole Porter, Coleman Hawkins."

"Will you play them for me?"

"If you come to Israel, I play everything."

I smiled.

"You like the music?" Aviv asked, nodding his head to the rhythm.

"Very much."

He put his arm around my shoulder and pulled me close.

Eggs scrambled on the grill at the diner near my office. I was on lunch hour, and Aviv would be on a flight home to Israel before I got off work.

"Do you remember the train in Peru?" Aviv asked.

"That's when I fell in love with you," I said.

Aviv beamed. "I go back to sit with the Israelis, and Mihal says, 'So when's the marriage?'"

"Why didn't you tell me before?"

"I thought maybe it was too early."

"But you're leaving," I said.

"Maybe you come to Israel."

Aviv had left a message on my answering machine. "I hope you like the surprise," he said. I pushed open my bedroom door. A happy face of fruit smiled at me from the center of the mattress on the floor. There were apples as eyes, an orange as a nose, and a banana as a mouth. I lay on the bed, cupped my hand over one of the apples, and closed my eyes. I wanted to feel him, but all I had was the apple, the stem between my fingers and the cold surface in my palm.

I checked the mailbox every day for two weeks, finding bills or an empty box until his letter arrived. He sketched his face on the back of the envelope, his scruffy hipster hair, glasses, and goatee rendered in black ink. The letter was only half a page, a double-spaced paragraph typed in old-school Courier font. He told me how both sisters and his parents met him at Ben-Gurion Airport in Tel Aviv, how happy he was to see his family, even though he was already annoyed with Revital. She could not find the dozen or more rolls of film he had sent to her for safekeeping, the rolls with his shots of Argentina, Chile, Brazil, and Bolivia, all of the places he'd been before we met in Peru. He had saved every ticket stub, postcard, and memento from the trip to document his journey in a series of albums. What good would they be without the photos? Despite the missing film, he was glad to be home. He was surprised that he didn't feel the letdown so many Israelis describe after their foreign travels. He thought he'd feel trapped in a tiny country with short buildings and small-minded people. He felt just fine.

The letter was full of spelling and grammatical errors, which I found so endearing that I never mentioned them. He described how hot he "fell" when he arrived in Tel Aviv on a steamy day wearing the fleece-lined leather coat he had "both" in Peru, words he would continue to write instead of *bought* and *feel*. He was living with his parents and studying for his college entrance exams, which he had to ace in order to get into the Technion. He recorded temperature fluctuations and listed the number of rainy days since he'd been home. At the end he said he loved me and missed me. I turned the letter over to make sure he had not written on the back. He hadn't.

I felt sleepy after a big Thanksgiving dinner of turkey, stuffing, mashed potatoes and gravy, green bean casserole, candied yams, pumpkin pie, and my father's cranberry relish. He ran cranberries, pineapple, an apple, an orange, and walnuts through a hand-operated meat grinder. I was in Connecticut, watching college football with my family, when the phone rang. It was on the other side of the room, a large family room in the basement off the deck to our backyard, and nobody moved. My mother finally got up and answered the phone.

She held out her arm and looked at me. "It's for you."

"Who is it?"

"Aviv."

I walked over and picked up the phone.

"How are you?"

"I miss you."

"I miss you, too."

"Can you come to Israel?"

"Now?"

"You can go on a kibbutz or maybe work as a waitress."

"I can't leave my job until I get into graduate school."

"You come for a visit?"

"I can't come now."

"Then when?"

"Maybe in February, after I apply to grad school."

"How long do you come?"

"I only have two weeks a year."

"This is nothing."

"I know."

I hung up and went back to the football game. My mother seemed wide awake.

"How's Aviv?"

"He misses me."

My mother nodded her head. "He wants you to come over there."

"That's what he wants."

"And?"

"I don't want to talk about it."

My mother hadn't taken to Aviv. The first time they met, he didn't get up and shake her hand or my grandmother's. Lulalee was in New York for the fiftieth reunion of the Radio City Rockettes. Glamorous as ever, she was a dark-haired beauty with movie star cheekbones and slanted blue eyes. The tallest dancer at five-foot seven, she was in the middle of the chorus line photo showcased at Radio City Music Hall when we went to the Christmas Spectacular. That summer, when she and my mother came to my apartment for a short visit, Aviv didn't get up. He sat in front of the television watching the news; something had come on about Israel, and Aviv made a sarcastic remark about the coverage. My mother wasn't a fan of his sarcasm. "He's sarcastic, just like my father. I can't stand sarcasm!"

My mother wasn't a fan of his long hair, either. It had grown down to his shoulders by the end of summer, when we took the commuter train to Connecticut to have dinner with my parents. We went to a steakhouse. "This is Karol's favorite restaurant. She likes the salad bar," my father chuckled.

Aviv blanched as he looked at the steaks on the grill

near our table. He ordered the salad bar, and while waiting for our steaks, my mother tried to talk to Aviv about computers, the way she talked to my brother, a computer systems engineer. She had been a math student at the University of Nebraska, packing candy for Russell Stover at night and going to school during the day. But she began to fall asleep in class, and after her second year in college, she dropped out to support my father through his last two years of engineering school, taking a full-time job in the agricultural school's computer statistics lab, programming a small mainframe computer in Fortran to analyze marbling, weight gain, and other beef cattle data, finding that the fattier, the tastier.

"I don't know hardwares, only softwares," Aviv said, responding to my mother's effort at conversation like a semi-mute teenage boy.

When my father's mother—a petite Scandinavian who wore her long silver-gray hair in two braids wrapped on her head like a crown—came to visit, she asked about Aviv.

"What does he look like?"

My father thought for a moment and said, "Jesus."

7

Sabra

"Passport," the Israeli guard said.

I was in Amsterdam, about to board my connecting flight to Tel Aviv. I set my passport down on the podium. The guard leafed through it to find a free page. There were visas and stamps on all but the last two. A roadmap of my year in South America. I now had visas for Israel and Egypt, too. I hoped to visit the pyramids.

The guard stopped flipping pages when he got to the Egyptian visa. He pinched his brow.

"Where do you stay in Israel?" he said.

"Haifa," I said.

"Who do you stay with?"

"My boyfriend."

His blue eyes interrogated. "Where do you meet your boyfriend?"

"Peru."

His eyes narrowed. "You meet in Peru?"

My stomach clenched. What was he thinking? A Palestinian boyfriend? A terrorist?

"How do you meet?"

"Backpacking."

"How long do you know him?"

"Almost a year."

"You are carrying something that is not yours?"

"No." I lied. I was carrying a package for Yael, the sister of Aviv's brother-in-law. She was living in New York City, and she had given me a package to deliver to her parents. I hadn't asked about the contents of the small package wrapped with a brown paper bag. Yael had told me that I should not tell the guard about the package because he might think it was a bomb. She had said not to worry about lying to the guard. It was a lie most Israelis told.

Aviv pulled off the coastal highway and headed down a quiet street filled with stucco ranch homes. We were in Kiryat Bialik, one of the suburbs of Haifa. It was named after the poet Hayyim Nahman Bialik. Aviv had told me about Bialik and other famous Zionists, like Theodor Herzl, author of *The Jewish State*. Aviv had given me a copy during our first months together, back in New York. He wanted me to know that Herzl, an Austrian journalist at the turn of the twentieth century, was the father of Zionism—the fundamental philosophy behind the development of a Jewish state, like Israel. Aviv told me that early on Herzl favored the Uganda Project—which was actually in Kenya—but Africa could not compete with the biblical roots in Palestine.

Aviv pointed to a five-story stucco apartment complex

beyond the intersection. "This is my home," he said. He pulled into a gravel driveway and parked under a covered patio. "Come, I show you my garden."

He led me across the patio to his garden. "I make all this," he said, pointing to ivy, orange nasturtiums, and cactuses. The cactuses looked like cucumbers, long as big baguettes. They leaned at odd angles against the stucco wall. He patted one of the cactuses. "Always I am coming to this garden, caring for these boys."

"How long?" I said.

"Since I am a child." He picked a few weeds, rescued a nasturtium caught under an ivy leaf, and propped up one of the cactuses against the stucco wall. It leaned over, as if it might uproot. "I'm caring for it every day."

"*Yofi*," I said, using the Hebrew word for "beauty." It was one of the first words I learned in the language because Aviv said it all the time in South America, taking photos of me and the lime-green Andes on our way to Machu Picchu.

Aviv squeezed my hand. "Come, we meet my parents." He grabbed my backpack, and I followed him up to the fourth floor. He pointed to the ceramic tile on the front door and ran his hand across the letters, moving from right to left, the way the language read. Backwards to me.

"Ben-Artzi," he said.

Aviv had told me that his father changed his name to Ben-Artzi after arriving in Israel. He wanted a new beginning. So Moshe Mueller, who might have become Moshe Miller if he'd gone to America after the war, became Moshe Ben-Artzi, "Son of my land."

"A whole new alphabet, that's something else," I said.

"Come," Aviv said, as he opened the door to the apartment.

"Ima, Aba," Mother, Father, Aviv called. A short, balding man emerged from one of the rooms, and a petite blonde woman stepped into the living room from an alcove.

"*Zot* Karol," Aviv introduced me.

"Shalom," they said.

Sarah and Moshe smiled and shook my hand. But the conversation didn't go anywhere. Sarah's English was awkward, and Moshe didn't even try. He spoke six languages—French, German, Hebrew, Russian, Romanian, and Yiddish—but he only spoke a few words of English and Spanish, the two languages I knew best. I already knew so much about them. Moshe and Sarah were both from Chernovitsi—a Ukrainian city that was part of Romania back then. Moshe was from a middle-class religious family, but he was an atheist like Aviv. At nineteen, he was arrested for his socialist-Zionist activism and sent to the Gulag, when Soviet troops invaded at the beginning of World War II. Moshe survived on bread and broth until his release after the war. Aviv said that his father would always push food, like an Italian grandmother. "Have some bread, eat, eat," he would say. Aviv was such a light eater, but Moshe would push anyway. He never wanted anyone to go hungry.

Sarah was ten years younger than Moshe, and she did not know him while they were growing up in Chernovitsi. Aviv wasn't sure about his mother's story: he thought she had come from a wealthy family that owned horses, and that her father and brother had been sent to Auschwitz in Poland, where Romanian-born writer Elie Wiesel was deported from Transylvania. But Chernovitsi was in another region, northern Bukovina, where Jews were

deported to Transnistria—the "Romanian Auschwitz"—
across the Dniester River in what is now Moldova. Aviv was
the youngest child, and by the time he was born, nobody
spoke of their deaths. He said that the silence made their
stories fester, wounds that never healed.

Aviv's bedroom was small, like a college dormitory. His bed
was as narrow as a cot with a thin foam cushion resting
on a storage trunk. It was more of a couch than a bed. It
took up half of the floor space. Later, Moshe, Sarah, Aviv,
and I would huddle in that room, wearing gas masks, as
Iraq shelled Israel with Scuds. Some would fall in Haifa,
only a handful of miles away from us. But we didn't know
that then. Saddam Hussein would not invade Kuwait for
six months.

A Martin Luther King photograph hung above the bed.
It was a black-and-white bust shot of King delivering his
famous speech, "I Have a Dream." Aviv liked that dream.
He had a dream, too, that his people would live in peace
with the Palestinians and all neighbors near and far. He
wanted true peace—not just the paper kind—with Egypt,
Jordan, and Lebanon, maybe even Syria, Iran, and Iraq,
and true peace in Israel, the land of milk and honey, the
place where the desert bloomed.

Aviv had never known peace. His mother chose the name
Aviv, the Hebrew word for "spring," because he arrived in
springtime—two months before the Six-Day War in June
1967, when Israel occupied the West Bank, the Golan Heights,
Gaza, and the Sinai Peninsula in a preemptive strike against
Egypt, Syria, and Jordan. Aviv was five when Black September, a Palestinian terrorist group, slaughtered eleven Israeli

athletes at the 1972 Munich Olympics. A year later, Egypt and Syria launched a surprise attack against Israel on Yom Kippur. He was twelve when Israel signed a peace agreement with Egypt, but that only brought cold peace.

Aviv wanted the kind of peace he imagined on a sheep farm in New Zealand, the kind he cultivated in his garden, the kind Martin Luther King talked about. That didn't come. Instead, when Aviv was a teenager, Fatah—the military arm of the Palestine Liberation Organization, the PLO—shelled Israel from southern Lebanon, and Israel invaded to create a "buffer zone." By the time Aviv finished his mandatory military service, the Palestinians had begun their uprising in occupied Gaza and the West Bank.

As much as Aviv yearned for peace, he feared it was an impossible dream. If the Israelis returned too much land, Aviv said that civil war might break out in his country, and it might not bring lasting peace with the Palestinians either. They had rejected the 1947 United Nations partition plan, and some still rejected the idea of dividing the country, hoping for the right of return for all Palestinians. Aviv said that his government would never allow that because Israel would no longer be a Jewish state. It wasn't a religious battle, Aviv said; it was a battle over the land. The West Bank and Gaza are not much bigger than Delaware, and Israel is about the size of New Jersey.

Aviv hoped anyway. So did I.

"Like the photo," I said.

"You know me, I'm for peace," he said.

Aviv's reverence for Martin Luther King wasn't just a political thing. It was part of his big infatuation with black America. Spike Lee, Michael Jordan, and all the jazz greats:

Oscar Peterson, Coleman Hawkins, Billie Holiday, Miles Davis, Charles Mingus. When he played pickup basketball games in Harlem, he'd get looks, at first: Who's this white guy? But he could play, and that's what counted.

Aviv drove to Mount Carmel, overlooking the port of Haifa. He parked the car at an observation deck, and we watched gray tankers rock in the harbor. "This is where the ships come at night," he said. He meant the ships carrying Jewish refugees from the Holocaust that would enter Haifa's port late at night and sneak past British troops. I watched waves lapping into hulls, as if the water held the secrets of history.

Aviv leaned against the railing of the observation deck above the port. "Come, I must show you my country," he said.

The sun burned my face—and the sand, my feet—as Aviv and I walked along the beach. We were in Eilat, an Israeli resort at the mouth of the Red Sea, where Israel meets Egypt and Jordan. The sea wasn't red. It was Caribbean blue. Israeli women lay topless on the beach, a statement that Israel was not one of the fundamentalist countries in the Middle East, no matter how much the religious right tried to make it so.

"You go topless?" Aviv pinched my shoulder.

I looked down at my one-piece suit. "How?" I said.

"Come." We walked over to a snorkel rental shop on the beach.

We held our masks and waded into the cool water. Saltwater stung my skin.

"Go under," Aviv said, pulling my hand.

Submerged, the sound of ocean pulsed through my ears. I kicked my fins, arms hanging loose at my sides. Breathing through my mouth. Plugging up my nose. Listening to air funnel down the snorkel, like a whale's spout, sucking in, pumping out. Parrot fish swam among spongy coral on the seabed, so shallow the waterline only reached my waist when standing up. The fish flashed like neon signs, striped in fluorescent blue, yellow, green, and pink. Bright as a pack of Magic Markers.

Aviv and I drove across the Egyptian border into the Sinai Peninsula. The Egyptian guard checked our passports and waved us through. We hiked to the top of a sandy hill. Across the Red Sea, the hills of Jordan and Saudi Arabia glistened pink.

"Sure you don't want to go to the pyramids?" I looked down the coast as if I might catch a glimpse of them.

"It's not safe," he said.

"Worse than Peru?"

"Last week, terrorists go onto a tour bus near Cairo and start shooting. Nine Israelis die, and seventeen are wounded."

We drove north. Sandstone pillars rose in the Timna Valley like those on the way to Petra, across the border in Jordan. Ibexes leapt over crevices in Negev Desert cliffs and roamed the Ein Gedi oasis. Salt clusters could have been icebergs in the Dead Sea. Camels, sheep, and Bedouins crossed dusty plains at Beersheba. A Scandinavian backpacker read the Bible by the Sea of Galilee. Israeli Arabs wore keffiyehs, prayed in mosques, and smoked nargilehs along the cobblestone streets of Akko. An Israeli soldier guarded the border with Lebanon, and because of a 1974 terrorist attack, a barbed-wire fence enclosed the kibbutz at the base of the Golan Heights where Moshe and Sarah had lived.

We drove south again, and in Tel Aviv off-duty soldiers strolled through the streets with M16s slung over their shoulders. Many of them were young men and women, fresh out of high school, doing their mandatory military service. A coed group sipped espresso at a sidewalk café. Their M16s lay on the table like pickup sticks.

"I've never seen so many guns," I said.

"When you're in the army, you can't go anywhere without your gun," Aviv said.

"What about the beach or a wedding?"

"Everywhere."

Inside the walls of the Old City of East Jerusalem, Christians lit candles at the Church of the Holy Sepulchre. Orthodox Jews in black hats and robes stuffed prayer scrolls into the Western Wall. Men rocked back and forth, murmuring prayers into the stones. An Israeli guard watched over them from the ramp leading to the Temple Mount. The guard rifled through our daypacks before letting us pass into the Muslim quarter. There, men left loafers at the door and kneeled inside the Al-Aqsa Mosque across from the Dome of the Rock. Women strolled through the stone courtyard in head wraps and long shifts.

"Come, we go this way," Aviv said, taking my hand. "But remember, check your back." He said that a British tourist, traveling through the West Bank, had been stabbed by a Palestinian.

We pushed through a steel door into a dim maze of cobblestone tunnels. It was so dark compared to the high desert sun in the courtyard. Corrugated aluminum gates closed like garage doors over all the stores.

"This place is usually very colorful," Aviv said.

The market sold everything from pastries to Palestinian clothes, rugs, saddlebags, ceramics, and souvenirs of olive wood, silverwork, mother-of-pearl, and hand-blown glass. It was early afternoon, but the shops had already closed because of the intifada—the shaking off—sparked when an Israeli truck crashed into a line of vans carrying Palestinian workers. Four men from a refugee camp in Gaza were killed, and protest erupted at the funeral over the deaths, the Israeli occupation, and the growth of Jewish settlements in the occupied land. The PLO called for general strikes and the boycott of Israeli goods, and merchants were doing their part to pressure the Israeli government to withdraw from the West Bank and Gaza. Palestinians who didn't go along with the protest were punished, and those who collaborated with the Israeli military were killed.

I heard footsteps behind us, swung around, and saw a Palestinian man wearing a keffiyeh. His face was like rawhide. He shuffled by in worn-out black loafers, the kind stacked outside the Al-Aqsa Mosque, hunched over as if he were carrying a load of sticks on his back.

Aviv pushed open a door.

I rubbed my eyes. The sun was bright. "Where are we?"

"The Jewish quarter. Now we eat a falafel."

A wiry man with dark curls stuffed falafel balls into

pitas and doused them with tahini. He scooped up the sandwiches, went into a back room, returned shortly, and handed us lunch.

Aviv pointed to a bench along the stone path. He looked ashen. "Why does he take the sandwiches to the back?"

I shrugged and sat down on the bench. "I don't know."

"There was a guy who almost dies from poison in a falafel."

"You mean the sandwich was poisoned on purpose?"

Aviv nodded yes. He cupped the pita in his hand, rusty-brown fried falafel balls popping out of its mouth.

"Was the guy who sold us the sandwiches Palestinian?" I said. The vendor had dark hair, almond eyes, olive skin, a long nose. I'd seen Israelis with the same features.

"Yes, he is Palestinian."

"But how did you know?"

"You live in Israel all your life, this is one thing you know."

"Should I eat the sandwich?"

Aviv bit into the falafel. "At least we die together." He laughed.

"Do you think we can see the Pool of Siloam?"

"That's beyond the Old City. Why do you want to see it?"

"It's where Jesus healed the blind man. I learned about it in Sunday school."

"But with the intifada, it's too dangerous."

"You never worried about terrorists in Peru."

"If you want to see this one place, then we go there, but we don't stay long."

"I wish we could see the rest of the West Bank."

Aviv shook his head. "It's not a good time."

I would have toured the entire West Bank if Aviv would have agreed. I had been afraid sometimes in South America, watching the mothers of those who went missing during the "dirty war" march in Buenos Aires, crossing the border into Pinochet's Chile and writing "journalist" as my profession, trekking through the Peruvian Andes wondering if I'd get kidnapped by a guerrilla. But nothing had happened to me, and by now I had the hunger of a war correspondent, driven by curiosity into exotic terrain full of conflict. I thought I could walk in the fiery furnace like Shadrach, Meshach, and Abednego and not get burned.

The cab wound down the hill, out of the Old City, farther into the West Bank. The earth looked parched as a desert. Trampled weeds scattered about bone-colored dust as far as I could see. No fertilized lawns. No gardens of nasturtiums. Barefoot children scampered toward the cab. Ragged little children and preteens. The driver crept by them, as if he worried about running over their shoeless feet. A boy picked up a stone, pulled his arm back as if getting ready to pitch, and hurled the rock at our cab. *Thump.* It hit the trunk, loud as thunder inside the car. The boy looked at us through the rear window, squinting his black eyes, punching his fists in the air, triumphant.

The driver stopped at a tunnel carved into stone. "That is your pool," he said.

"You wait for us?" Aviv asked the driver.

He nodded yes.

A sign—small as a KEEP OFF THE GRASS sign, stuck in the dirt near the entrance—read POOL OF SILOAM. I had imagined a big pool, something grand like the Trevi Fountain in Rome or the Bethesda Fountain in Central Park in New York City. I never imagined a dark, damp tunnel.

"Is the taxi driver Palestinian?" I asked.

"Yes."

"Oh."

A pool of water blocked our path. A moist draft chilled me.

"That's your famous pool," Aviv said.

"It's not at all what I expected," I said. "Not at all."

We waited for a bus in the central terminal in West Jerusalem, the modern part of the city. Soldiers in olive uniforms mingled with Orthodox Jews and secular civilians on the platform. As I leaned against the wall, sipping a can of Coca-Cola, a guard bellowed into a megaphone.

"What is he saying?" I asked.

"He wants us to move." Aviv took my hand.

Everyone moved to the other side of the parking lot, taking cover behind a large red Egged bus. I peered around the front of the bus to see what was happening. An army bag remained alone on the platform.

"They worry it's a bomb," Aviv said.

"A bomb?"

A midnight-blue-and-white jeep sounding a loud siren sped toward the platform. A robot fetched the bag.

A convoy of taxis rolled toward us. Drivers leaned out the window shouting destinations, "Tel Aviv? Haifa?"

"The guy will charge double," Aviv said.

"Look," I nudged Aviv.

A red Egged bus pulled into the parking lot. One of the windows had shattered like a spiderweb.

"That bus is coming from the Old City," Aviv said.

I looked at the shattered window, and thought of the boy who'd thrown the stone at our cab, poisoned falafel sandwiches, tourists gunned down in Egypt, the British traveler stabbed in the West Bank, and how Israelis tried to prevent it all with soldiers and rules, like reserving seats for Israeli military in the front of buses; calling for security bars around bus drivers' seats to keep terrorists from jerking the steering wheel and sending the bus tumbling into a ditch; giving Palestinians from Gaza and the West Bank blue, green, and white license plates, rather than yellow plates like Israeli citizens; making cars with blue, green, and white plates return to the occupied territories before evening curfews; requiring Palestinians over sixteen to carry identity cards and stopping cars and inspecting IDs at military checkpoints; shooting rockets and real and rubber bullets; sealing and bulldozing homes; plowing olive grows; and building a reinforced-concrete wall along the West Bank. The Palestinians fought back with Molotov cocktails, rockets, shootings, stabbings, stones, and, later, suicide bombs.

Aviv sighed. "You see how it is to live in Israel. It is a pressure cooker. This is why I am always dreaming of a sheep farm in New Zealand. But New Jersey I'm thinking isn't so bad."

Aviv and I sat in a patch of crown anemones, their crimson blooms peppering the rocky green hills of northern Israel. Aviv reached into his backpack and pulled out a bag of green cactus pears—*sabras*.

"Now you try your first *sabra*," Aviv said as he peeled the skin. "You know, we call Israelis who are born here *sabras*. This is because we are prickly on the outside, sweet on the inside."

I bit into the soft pink *sabra*. It tasted something like a kiwi. Bittersweet.

"You like *sabras*?" he asked as he peeled another.

I smiled and kissed him on the cheek. "Yes." I always liked warm people who didn't sugarcoat, who told the truth. Thorny, brutal, and bare.

"We come here when I am a child," Aviv said, running his fingers over the wildflowers.

"It's so beautiful," I said.

"Families come here for picnics. I think I bring my family here when I have one."

An image came into focus: Aviv and me and our two children, a boy and girl. Close in age, one with lemon hair like Sarah's and another with chestnut hair like Aviv's. All four of us sitting there, among the crimson anemones and boulders and spiky grass, nibbling on peeled prickly pears, listening to Aviv tell us stories about his life as a *sabra*. It would be a good life, I thought. I didn't worry about the intifada. I took notes and wrote about it when I got home. I still hadn't experienced war, and the terror that seeps into your blood, when you come to realize that you are not immune.

8

Give Peace a Chance

Aviv finished his year as a student at the University of Haifa and came back to New York to live with me. He worked for Israeli moving companies—Moishe's, Noah's Ark, and Schleppers—like he had when we first met. But he complained about the bruises, gashes, sore muscles, filthy apartments, and rude customers. "I feel like a second-class citizen," he said. He'd lost patience for that kind of work. He was a diligent student with plans for graduate school, like me. I had been accepted to the Columbia University School of International and Public Affairs, but I soon switched to the School of Journalism, where I'd earn my master's degree. By now, Aviv had decided to study sociology at the University of Haifa instead of computer science at the Technion, eventually transferring to the City College of New York, where he'd earn a combined bachelor's and master's degree. Later, he would finish his PhD and become a professor.

Aviv took a slow sip of his cappuccino, set the cup down,

and stared at the white foam. "Tell me something," he said, still looking into the cup, "Do you take your children to church?"

"I don't go to church anymore," I said.

He pushed his glasses up the bridge of his nose. "But if you have children, do you take them to church?"

I put my hand on his. "Do you want me to convert?"

He shook his head. "No, no, you know how I am not believing in God. I don't want my children going to temple or church."

"But how do you teach moral values without religion?"

Aviv waved his hand. "This is nonsense. People don't need religion to learn to be civilized."

"So, if I don't bring my children to church, will you teach them to be civilized?"

"Okay."

Aviv and I stretched out on my bed reading the *New York Times* when the phone rang. It was Andy. We'd met at my night job, a part-time gig I'd keep through graduate school, writing news briefs for a broadcast-news clip service in Times Square. Aviv and I had been together for almost a year and a half by now, but we'd spent most of that winter and spring apart, except for our three weeks together in Israel. Aviv had said we should date other people while we were apart, but Aviv never went out with anyone else, making long and expensive phone calls several times a week, sending packages with tender letters and sketches of his face and hair and goatee on the envelope and mixed tapes full of love songs like Sinéad O'Connor's "Nothing Compares 2 U."

I hadn't wanted to see anyone else, but knowing that Aviv was only coming for the summer and would leave again by fall, I finally gave in to the craving for company. Talk came easily with Andy, an aspiring writer who showed up for our first date with George Orwell's *Homage to Catalonia* tucked into the cargo pocket of his jacket, but being with him underscored how much I wanted Aviv. Later, when I told Aviv about Andy, he said, "But I thought if you loved me you wouldn't want to go out with anyone else."

When I hung up, Aviv asked, "Who was that?"

"Andy."

Aviv grimaced. "You let that guy call here?"

"I have to have friends. You're leaving, remember?"

"He doesn't want to be your friend. He wants to have sex with you!"

I stood by the bed, arms crossed. "We should just break up until we can live together."

Aviv stared at me, watery eyes. "If we break up, I can't reopen my feelings for you."

I began to sob. "It's all or nothing. That's not fair. You're leaving!"

"I want to wait until I finish with school, but I must say this, I want you to be my wife."

"You want to get married?"

"I want that you come to Israel with me and that we marry. So you are saying yes?"

"Yes, I'm saying yes."

I'd known all along that I wanted to marry Aviv, who'd felt like a best friend from the beginning. He was an unusually good listener, patient, compassionate, wise, and witty, who made me feel like his equal. He was good-looking, athletic, and confident, sometimes to the point of cocky, but this I found endearing because he was so gentle and nurturing, always making coffee and avocado and olive sandwiches, always holding my hand wherever we went. He was a good negotiator, rational and even-keel, a comfort to my more impulsive and passionate nature. He was an idealist, who had big dreams about peace so that someday he could travel to Petra with an Israeli passport, so that someday Israel might have lasting peace. He was also a realist, a doubter, and a pessimist, knowing how hard it would be to achieve. But Aviv was above all a humanist, who saw beyond race and religion and nationality, who saw that at the core we are all the same. This view of humanity was the cement of our cross-cultural relationship. It was our faith, our religion.

I had no hesitation when Aviv asked me to move to Israel to get to know his family, his culture, his language, before we married and moved back to New York, where we both could go to school. Our plan seemed simple enough. Aviv would spend the year studying at the University of Haifa, and I'd defer graduate school, work on a kibbutz, and learn Hebrew. But Columbia said no. I could not defer admission. I had to attend for at least one semester before I could take time off. So I had to stay in New York, while Aviv went back home, and this last separation felt like an indignity.

It was the summer of 1990, and things had begun to heat up in the Middle East. Saddam Hussein got into a dispute with Kuwait over oil: he accused the Kuwaitis of tapping Iraqi oil by drilling at a slant and depressing oil prices through overproduction. Iraq had run up a huge debt during its decade-long war against Iran, and Saddam

Hussein looked hungrily at his wealthy neighbor and creditor. Iraq sent troops to the Kuwaiti border in July, and on the first day of August, Iraqi soldiers invaded the country. The United Nations imposed economic sanctions against Iraq and occupied Kuwait, to pressure Saddam Hussein to withdraw peacefully from Kuwait. But fear had spread that Iraq might invade Saudi Arabia, too. And within days of the invasion, a coalition of countries led by the United States began sending troops and supplies to the Middle East, preparing to defend Saudi Arabia and push the Iraqi military out of Kuwait. If the coalition attacked, Saddam Hussein threatened to fire chemical and biological weapons at Israel, hoping to draw Israel into the war and break up the broad coalition of countries that included many in the Middle East—Egypt, Syria, Saudi Arabia, Kuwait, Bahrain, Oman, Qatar, the United Arab Emirates, Morocco, Turkey, Pakistan, and Bangladesh—as well as nations all over the world.

Ofra Haza, an Israeli singer, went to the United States to make a recording and music video of "Give Peace a Chance," John Lennon's antiwar song, which came out in 1969 at the height of the Vietnam War. The remake, produced by Lenny Kravitz, featured Lennon's son Sean and more than twenty artists such as Bonnie Raitt, M.C. Hammer, Peter Gabriel, and LL Cool J. I hoped that sanctions and diplomacy would work, but it did not look good. This kind of war worried me. Somehow, I always thought that I could talk down a Shining Path warrior or a stone-throwing boy. But a Scud filled with toxic chemicals? How could I talk my way out of that?

Aviv called and sounded blue. He was in London, visiting Revital, who was living there.

"Have you been watching the news?" I said.

"Saddam Hussein has great timing," he said.

"Are you worried about a war?"

"No, this is just talk—Saddam Hussein is not so crazy to attack Israel. What, and go against the best air force in the world?"

"Then why do you sound so down?"

"My sister, she does not approve."

While living in New York, Revital had met a man from San Francisco who wanted to marry her. Aviv said, "The guy had a big house and looked like Tom Selleck." But he wasn't Jewish, and Sarah had said no. So Revital went back to Israel and still had not married. When I first heard the story, I worried, but Aviv assured me that he would "handle his parents." So far, they had not protested, probably because I was going to Israel. We had not expected it from Revital.

Revital was hip, and she was good to Aviv. He used to spend weekends at her apartment in Tel Aviv when he was in high school. Sarah would sigh and say, "Aviv picks Revital for a mother." When she visited us in New York, she turned to me the day before she left and said, "Make sure he cuts his hair." It was an order. When I went to Israel for the first time, Revital cornered me in the kitchen on my last night. "If you go back to New York, you will break my brother's heart." I admired Revital for her boldness, but I feared her the way I feared my own mother. It was a relief that she was in London, working for the Israeli government as a cultural liaison, and she would not come back to Israel until the war was over.

Not long after that, Aviv discovered that Israeli rabbis do not perform interfaith marriages, and that the government has no provision for civil marriages. If we wanted to marry in Israel, I would have to convert with an Orthodox rabbi. Aviv, an atheist and a humanist, was against my conversion. Instead, we could fly to Cyprus for a quick ceremony, or we could apply for a proxy marriage through the embassy of Paraguay. It would cost about a thousand dollars. We decided to wait until we got back to New York. "I don't know my country as well as I'm thinking," Aviv said. Despite these setbacks—and the unsettling possibility of war—I still planned to fly to Israel after my first semester of graduate school. I booked a flight for January 15, which turned out to be the United Nations' deadline for Iraq to withdraw from Kuwait. Airlines began canceling flights to Israel and other spots in the Middle East, but the Dutch airline KLM continued to fly. I moved the flight up a week.

Aviv called before I was about to leave and sounded down—again.

"My mother thinks you should not come. She thinks there will be war."

"I know, but I miss you. I don't want to wait it out in New York."

On the airplane, I sat next to a man with salt-and-pepper hair, a thick shock of it. He wore tortoise-shell glasses and a hunter-green sweater vest. "A young American heading to Europe, a backpack trip, I suppose?" He sounded British.

"Actually, I'm going to Israel."

His right eyebrow peaked above his glasses. "You're quite a brave young lady."

I shrugged.

"I think Israel's going to use this war to take more land."

"I hope Saddam Hussein leaves Israel out of it."

The marbled-glass door to Aviv's bedroom was closed. It had become the sealed room. We slept in Moshe's study instead, pushing his two slim couches together like a double bed. I lay awake gazing at Moshe's library in the dim light. There were hundreds of books filling every nook. A room filled floor to ceiling, wall to wall, with books. Burgundy, brown, and black. Leather books that made me wonder about all their contents, how much Aviv's father must know from reading them. Moshe was a high school history teacher who had written a textbook about democracy, and now he was writing his memoir about surviving the Gulag. I got out of bed and ran my hand across a row of books. I noticed Karl Marx's *Communist Manifesto*. I pulled it off the shelf. It was in German.

In the morning, Moshe knocked on the study door and told us breakfast was ready.

"Shalom," I said as I walked into the kitchen behind Aviv.

"Shalom," Sarah said. "You have good sleep?"

"Yes, thank you."

"Sit, sit," Moshe said, directing Aviv and me to the kitchen table.

Sarah had prepared scrambled eggs, diced tomato and cucumber salad, toast, and Turkish coffee. It was a typical Israeli breakfast.

"Eat, eat," Moshe said in English. He nodded his head eagerly.

"Aviv tells me you have lived in South America," Sarah said.

"Yes, Argentina."

"I was in Chile." She smiled. "You speak Spanish?"

"Yes."

Sarah was a petite blonde with even features, ruddy cheeks, and smooth skin. She spoke to me in Spanish— intimately, as if I were one of her friends—about how she'd met a young man on the ship to Chile, how she'd danced with him every night, smiling as if remembering an old love.

"Moshe doesn't like dancing," Sarah said in Spanish.

Aviv looked at his father, busily eating his breakfast.

"Does Aviv like these things?" Sarah asked in Spanish.

"Ima," Aviv said.

I laughed and told her about our nights out in Manhattan, dancing to samba music while a Brazilian woman in a white satin gown crooned in Portuguese.

"Good, good." She smiled.

After Aviv left for the university, Moshe walked into the kitchen with pad and pencil. "*Ivrit*," he said, shaking the pad and pencil in the air. Moshe was a short, scholarly man, who dressed like a professor in V-neck sweaters and gray slacks. Nodding at him, I sat down at the kitchen table and began my first Hebrew lesson. Inches from me, Moshe wrote the alphabet on a notepad. He pointed to the first letter and said, "*Alef*." His finger moved to the second letter, and he said, "*Bet*." He went through the whole alphabet like that, pointing at unfamiliar shapes and pronouncing letters. Then he had me practice writing the letters—*alef*, *bet*, *gimel*, *dalet*.

Some of the shapes were difficult for me, and this seemed to frustrate Moshe. He'd grab the pencil from me and correct my mistakes. His voice sounded stern, like an old-world schoolmaster, as if I were a poor student who had to be prodded to learn lessons. I nearly wept. Hours later, Sarah stepped into the kitchen and snapped at Moshe in Hebrew. I don't know what she said, but he picked up the pad and pencil and walked out of the kitchen. Timidly, I went to the study, wrote in my journal, and took a nap.

That night, Aviv took me to the Israeli Civil Defense office to get a gas mask. The line extended from the basement office up to the sidewalk and down the block. We got in line. I had not expected the crowd. The United Nations deadline for Iraq to withdraw from Kuwait was only a handful of days away, and I thought that most Israelis would already have received their masks.

"Why so many people?" I said.

"Maybe some people were thinking there wouldn't be war," Aviv said.

Israelis chatted in Hebrew, and though I did not understand, I felt the calm rhythm of the speech. I looked at the faces. Boredom, the kind of blank stares people have waiting in long lines at a bank or a bus terminal. Then I heard a man speaking in Spanish behind me. A tall man with leathery skin and salt-and-pepper hair, he told the woman beside him that he worried he would not get a mask; he wasn't Israeli, and he didn't speak Hebrew or English.

"You'll get a mask," I told him in Spanish.

His eyes widened. "You speak Spanish?"

"I'm from the United States, but I lived in Argentina," I said.

He smiled. "I'm from Chile. I'm not Jewish, so I worry maybe I won't get a mask."

"Don't worry, they have to give everybody masks, even the Palestinians in the West Bank."

"This is true?" the man asked.

"Yes, you'll get a mask," Aviv said in Spanish.

The Israeli Supreme Court, which Aviv said was the true voice of democracy in his country, had ordered the Israeli Defense Forces to give gas masks to the 1.5 million Palestinians in the occupied territories. While distribution would turn out to be slow and incomplete—the country only had 173,000 extra masks, and the military was supposed to buy enough for everyone—I did not know that then.

The man raised his eyebrows, surprised. "He speaks Spanish, too?"

"Yes, we met in Peru." I said, smiling at Aviv.

"How beautiful," the man said.

"We'll be there to translate if you have any problems," I said.

"Thank you, young lady," he said, bowing his head.

"So how did you end up in Israel?" I asked the man.

"I work in the agricultural fields," he said.

"You came here with your family?"

"My wife," he said, resting his hand on her shoulder.

"He's my fiancé," I said, putting my arm around Aviv's waist.

"Don't worry, you will get your mask," Aviv said.

The line moved like molasses, turning from dusk to night as we waited. We inched toward the stairwell and finally made it inside the basement office. It was a small, bright room. A half-dozen guards dressed in olive fatigues sat behind a long table handing out gas mask kits. Finally, it was my turn, and I handed the guard my passport. He studied all of my stamps and visas and then snapped, "Okay, sign here." I signed the form, and the guard handed me a tan cardboard container with a black plastic shoulder strap. It looked like a cardboard lunchbox, the color of coffee and cream. The gas mask was inside.

"*Señorita*." The Chilean man tapped me on the shoulder.

He needed me to translate. After a few questions, the guard handed the man his mask. He held the box to his chest, looked down at it, and then at me, as if I'd saved his life.

"*Muchas, muchas gracias*." Many, many thanks, the man said in Spanish.

"*De nada*." You're welcome, I said.

That night, Aviv showed me how to use the gas mask. I opened the kit and dumped all of the contents on the bed. A tube of decontamination powder. An atropine syringe. A gas mask and filter, which fit to the mask like a snout. I held the mask in my hands, and following Aviv's instructions, I attached the filter, removed the cap, stretched the strap over my head, and secured the mask to my face, making sure it was airtight. I could barely breathe and jerked it off.

"How do you breathe under these things?" I asked Aviv.

"Breathe slowly, don't panic," he coached, gently, patiently.

At the time I only had a vague understanding of chemical and biological warfare. But years later, my father would tell me that when he was in chemical, biological, and radiological warfare school in the army, he watched a demonstration of how atropine was supposed to revive a goat after exposure to vx—a nerve agent developed in the United

Kingdom in the 1950s that causes muscle contractions and asphyxiation. The instructor released a single drop of liquid vx from an eyedropper onto the goat's neck. My father said that the goat went down instantly: "You could tell it was down for the count. It was stone dead." It had been through several demonstrations, and this time the atropine injected in the goat's shoulder didn't work. So the instructor explained that atropine loses its effectiveness after repeated exposure to nerve agents.

vx was one of a long list of chemical and biological toxins that United Nations weapons inspectors found in Iraq after the Gulf War, something I learned long after the war. Iraq's cache, tallied in a 1999 United Nations report, included anthrax, botulinum toxin, mustard gas, sarin, and tabun, among others. The most powerful chemical toxins are nerve agents—including sarin, tabun, and vx—which cause a runny nose, confusion, nausea, diarrhea, chest tightening, sweating, shaking, and suffocation, without a quick injection of atropine into muscles or veins. While vx is the most deadly of the three in its liquid form, it is as thick as motor oil and evaporates slowly. Sarin and tabun, developed as pesticides in Germany in the 1930s, evaporate much more quickly, increasing the likelihood that people will breathe the toxic vapors. Sarin has a fruity smell, but tabun and vx are odorless.

Mustard gas, a blister agent developed by Germany in 1917, was first used during World War I. It smells like garlic, onions, or mustard and causes the skin to blister and burn, turning blackish blue. There is no antidote for mustard gas, and though it isn't immediately fatal, it can cause second- and third-degree burns, blindness, lung disease, and respiratory failure without quick decontamination. According to Human Rights Watch, Iraq used mustard gas, sarin, and tabun to kill about twenty-two thousand Iranians and five thousand Kurds during the Iran-Iraq War, despite the 1925 Geneva Protocol banning chemical and germ warfare.

Botulinum toxin, sold commercially as Botox, is created by *Clostridium botulinum*—muscle-paralyzing bacteria that cause botulism. In its mildest form, it temporarily erases facial wrinkles, but it can also cause double vision, blurred vision, slurred speech, difficulty swallowing, dry mouth, muscle weakness, and respiratory failure without the use of a vaccine. And anthrax is an infectious disease caused by spore-forming bacteria that create blisters on the skin when touched; nausea, loss of appetite, bloody diarrhea, fever, and stomach pain when swallowed; and a cough, sore throat, mild fever, chest discomfort, shortness of breath, tiredness, and muscle aches when inhaled. Antibiotics can cure anthrax contracted through the skin, but the disease is deadlier when digested or breathed.

After the Gulf War, United Nations inspectors found seventy-five "special" Scud warheads filled with anthrax, botulinum toxin, sarin, and trace amounts of vx—though Saddam Hussein denied weaponizing vx. United Nations inspectors destroyed thirty of the warheads and accounted for the rest by excavating remains of those destroyed by Iraq in the wake of the Gulf War. Inspectors also found aerial bombs, rockets, and artillery shells laced with chemicals. The Iraqi Scud, a modified Soviet Scud-B renamed the Al Hussein, had a range of 650 kilometers, or 400 miles, and an explosive capacity equal to 250 kilograms, or 550 pounds, of TNT—about a seventh of the force used in the 1995 Oklahoma City bombing. But the Al Hussein was wildly imprecise: It only had a fifty-fifty chance of coming within one kilometer of its intended target. It was strategically ineffective, but a good weapon of terror. Under the right weather conditions—calm, clear skies—a single "special" Scud could kills hundreds, if not thousands, of unprotected people.

It is ironic that most of Saddam Hussein's chemical and biological weapons had been discovered and destroyed by United Nations weapons inspectors by the time the United States and its small list of allies toppled Saddam Hussein in 2003. United Nations weapons inspectors, who had been thrown out of Iraq in 1998, were allowed back in the country prior to the invasion, but they could not find any evidence of chemical, biological, or nuclear weapons. Neither could the United States military, which searched the country following the invasion. Rumors about illegal imports of yellowcake uranium and secret stocks of chemical and biological weapons turned out to be false, like much of the intelligence about Iraq's "weapons of mass destruction" leading up to the Iraq War.

Aviv sat at his desk working on the computer.

"I had a three-hour Hebrew class with your father today."

"Three hours?" Aviv asked.

I reached for my journal. "Can I read you what I've written?"

"Of course."

I wrote how Moshe reminded me of my violin teacher in high school, a stern Soviet émigré who would prod and prod and prod. "Not 99 percent, 100 percent," Asya would say all the time. Once, when I was arriving for my lesson, two elementary school girls ran toward their mother's car, bawling after their lesson. She made me cry sometimes, too, but the funny thing is that I liked her. Sometimes, when she had too many students back to back, she would sit me down in the kitchen, make Turkish coffee, and share stories. She told me how her mentor told her never to rush, so she never did; how she knew she was ready to perform when she was nervous, but she was in trouble when she was calm; and how she lost a prestigious orchestra job and thought her life was over until a friend said, "This is as bad as it gets, Asya. It only gets better."

9
Black Elephants

The air-raid siren went off in the middle of the night. It scaled high and low, over and over, warning us that Iraq had sent its first round of Scuds to Israel. Aviv and I bounded out of bed as if we'd already downed a pot of coffee, startled by the siren and thoughts of bombs hitting our apartment, warheads releasing deadly germs and gases. Aviv rushed down the hall to get his parents, while I hurried into the turtleneck, tights, socks, and boots I'd laid out for the raid and ran to the sealed room, a sprinter going for personal best. Aviv soon followed, clothed like me.

"I hope Saddam Hussein doesn't have such good luck that the bombs fall on the refineries. Half of Israel burns If he does that." The Haifa refineries were only few miles down the Mediterranean coast from us.

"*Bo'u henah*," Aviv called to his parents, urging them to come into the room.

Moshe and Sarah shuffled down the hall, still in their pajamas. They weren't prepared like Aviv and me. Sarah's nightgown only reached her knees, and both of them wore open-toed slippers, exposing bare feet. Why hadn't they covered themselves? Weren't they worried? The air-raid siren was plainly telling us that warheads were coming our way, warheads that might contain lethal things, but Moshe and Sarah ambled along, unalarmed. Later, I came to understand that as people who had lived through the Holocaust and all of Israel's wars after independence, this was just another war. But that night, I worried like an over-protective mother. Once Moshe and Sarah were in, Aviv slammed the door so hard I thought all the little marbled-glass squares would tumble to the floor. I imagined that door without any glass, just the wire grid.

Aviv didn't stop to notice. He shifted into overdrive as he reached under the bed for a towel, rolled it, and stuffed it along the bottom of the door. Then he grabbed thick, brown tape and spread it along the edge of the door. The room was sealed. I tried to move fast like Aviv. I pulled our gas mask kits from under the bed and dropped them on top. Aviv had printed our names on the cardboard boxes in black Magic Marker. I opened my box and reached in. The rubber mask chilled my hands. Inside the box, there was a clear plastic cylinder filled with decontamination powder that looked like talc. If chemicals beaded on my skin, I should sprinkle the powder. That seemed simple. But the atropine injector next to it frightened me. It had a long, thick needle that I should jab into my skin to release the nerve gas antidote. But I didn't know where to stick it. A vein, a thigh?

There was no time for questions now. I had to get that gas mask on. Aviv had made me practice, so I knew what to do. I removed the cap on the filter, screwed it onto the snout, and fit the mask to my face. I ran my fingers along the edge to make sure the seal was tight. Then I slid the strap over my head and pulled tight, but not too tight. I didn't want it to pinch and have to fiddle with it after the bombs had dropped. Moshe and Sarah fumbled with their masks. It seemed like they hadn't tried to put them on before. Moshe twisted the mask in his hands, furrowing his brow as he fit the mask to his face and the strap to the back of his head. Sarah watched how Moshe put on his mask, and then she put hers on, too, her hair bunching up above the strap. Moshe and Sarah sat on the bed, while Aviv and I sat on the cold, tile floor—knees bent into our chests, shoulders melding together, backs against the wall.

Aviv's bedroom had become the sealed room because it was the smallest in his parents' fourth-floor apartment, following the civil defense guidelines of sealing a small, above-ground room. The reinforced-concrete bomb shelter on the ground floor was good for a conventional attack, but not a chemical one, since gases settle on the ground. Of course, the sealed room wouldn't protect us if we took a direct hit. But the logic was comforting enough. The room's only window was covered with a clear plastic tarp, reinforced by packaging tape—a big brown X that would protect the tarp from tearing even if a bomb shattered the pane. The radio announcers kept repeating instructions in Hebrew and a series of languages—English, Russian, Amharic, Romanian, Yiddish, and French—to go to the sealed room, put on a gas mask, and stay put until the air raid was over. We waited to hear the all-clear siren, a flat tone, but all we heard were the announcers and the rise and fall of the air-raid siren blaring outside.

I turned to check the seal on Aviv's mask. I could see gaps because of his beard. He'd cropped it short, but that only made the seal a little tighter. It was supposed to be airtight, and it wasn't. I wished he would have shaved his beard, but he didn't want to take it off, and I hadn't pushed him to do it, either. Now I wished I had. After all, it wasn't as though he kept a beard for religious reasons, like the Orthodox. He'd only grown one because I'd wanted him to. We all had come into that room with our shortfalls. Aviv hadn't cut his beard. Moshe and Sarah hadn't covered their skin. I hadn't learned how to use the atropine syringe. It was too late to do better. All we could do was wait and listen.

I heard missiles burst—loudly, one after the other. I had not expected that. Somehow, I thought the bombs would land somewhere else, somewhere far away. I was wrong. I wondered what had been hit. A home, a school, a synagogue? I waited, fists clenched, pulse thumping against my skin, hoping the floor would not cave in, sucking Aviv and Moshe and Sarah and me into concrete abyss, praying I wouldn't hear the crackling inferno ripping up the coast if the refineries had been hit. I sniffed for chemicals, but the only odor was rubber, like the interior of a new car. My cheeks flushed, and nausea brewed in my gut. How long would I have to wait like this, hot and sick and suffocated under this rubber mask? I looked at Moshe and Sarah and Aviv, wondering if they felt like me. Cramped. Confined. Agitated. Afraid. I could see their eyes through the lens of the black rubber mask. Nervous like mine. We were no longer men and women. The mask was our hide, the filter, however short, our trunk. We were black elephants, stripped of our humanity, trapped like wild game.

Aviv jerked his black-shrouded head toward me and pointed at my mask. I looked down. Liquid beads formed on the snout like morning dew. Chemical contamination? Should I grab the powder? Nerve gas? Should I grab the syringe? My abdomen contracted so hard I thought I'd puke. I peered at Aviv through my Plexiglas lens. What should I do? I felt like I was free-falling without a parachute.

Aviv pointed to my snout and mumbled, his words as incoherent as a scuba diver's underwater. He kept pointing and repeating what sounded like "Whomp whomp, whomp whomp, whomp whomp," until I finally figured it out. "Your breath, your breath, your breath." The water beads might be my breath, condensed on the snout of my mask.

I nodded to let Aviv know that I understood, and he nodded back. We weren't absolutely sure that the dew-like beads were only my condensed breath, but that possibility offered such relief that we burst into laughter, quivering and quaking, barely a sound escaping the rubber smothering our mouths. We were like teenagers cutting up at a funeral.

We stopped, abruptly, when Moshe ripped off his mask. His cheeks were flushed, and he gulped, as if he'd been dunked underwater way too long. His chest heaved, swelling out and caving in, begging for air. I wanted to scream, "Don't take it off, we don't know what's in those warheads that fell." But I couldn't say any of that from under my mask. So I watched, silently, assuring myself that a man who'd survived the Gulag would survive this, too. As I stared, through the beady eyes of my mask, his chest stopped heaving, and his cheeks resumed their natural hue. I closed my eyes and prayed that Moshe and Sarah and Aviv and I would make it through the night unharmed.

I thought about my father, how early mornings in Vietnam he read the Bible and the Christian Science textbook, small leather-bound books he carried in the cargo pockets of his army shirt. My father began his tour as a forward observer with the infantry, calling in artillery rounds from the battery of howitzers when his company took fire. His men used to rib him about it until their helicopter flew off course and got shot down by the Viet Cong. None of the men remember what happened, but the pilot and copilot were safe in the cockpit of the mangled chopper, and the rest of the soldiers were scattered on the hillside, untouched. A bullet grazed my father's helmet when he peeked over the hilltop to figure out where they had crashed. After that, his men said, "Keep reading the good book."

The release siren went off, its monotone wail assuring us that the air raid was over, that it was safe to take off our gas masks and leave the sealed room. I lifted my mask, and the queasiness began to ease. Moshe and Sarah left their masks on the bed and rushed to the television. Aviv and I put them back in the cartons, stuffed them under the bed, and joined his parents. CNN was right there, filming everything—heaps of debris from buildings damaged in Haifa and Tel Aviv, apartments and homes missing walls, the wounded on stretchers being lifted into ambulances. I listened for reports of chemical and biological warfare, of how many had died. But all I heard were reports about concussions, gashes, shock, unnecessary atropine injections, heart attacks, asthma attacks, and suffocation. Four elderly Jewish women and an Arab girl had not removed caps from their filters and died as they struggled to breathe under their masks. Moshe had a heart condition and was scheduled to have an operation in six months, a typical wait under Israel's public health care system, but it seemed unbearably long at that moment, and Aviv would worry about him throughout the war.

After that first early-morning raid, the public was instructed to check masks for black rubber corks blocking the filter, and asthmatics were given priority to receive blowers—a less restrictive breathing device that looks like a clear, hooded poncho—that had been given to young children and later to some religious men who did not want to shave their beards. Aviv continued to use a gas mask throughout the war, even though he kept his beard, and the seal was never airtight.

Sarah ran to the telephone in Aviv's room and called Ofra, Aviv's middle sister, who lived with her husband and baby girl in Ramat Gan, a town near Tel Aviv that would take many hits during the war. Ofra's daughter, Nirit, used a plastic pup tent for babies instead of a gas mask.

I watched Sarah talk, a serious expression on her face, but I couldn't understand a word. When she hung up, she announced in Hebrew, "*Hakol beseder*." Everything is okay. It was one of the few phrases I knew.

Now it was my turn. I'd promised my mother that I

would call home after each air raid. I dialed and redialed to get an international operator. Each time I'd get a busy signal. When I finally got through, the operator sounded almost bored when she asked, "And where are you calling from?"

"Israel," I said.

"Israel? Really? I've had a lot people trying to call over there. You're my first call from Israel. What's it like?"

"It's over for now, I hope."

She gasped. "Imagine."

There was a short pause, then my mother picked up.

"I'm seeing some of the Scuds fell near Haifa," she said.

"Yeah, they sure sounded close," I laughed.

"Close call, huh?" she said.

I laughed because I'd had many close calls. Like the close call as a little girl when my mother saw me dart across the street toward an ice cream truck without checking for cars, bouncing off the front end of a big sedan as it drove by. Or the close call in junior high when she caught me riding my bike down the driveway, straight into traffic, without looking both ways. Or the close call as a teenager at summer camp in the Colorado Rocky Mountains when I caught my foot on a root at the top of a steep slope while sliding down to a stream, doing an accidental full-body flip and landing sure-footed in a small fish nest, the one smooth spot in the streambed.

My mother laughed, too, not because she took the war lightly, but because she had the trench humor of a soldier who knew the stress of war. She had always said that the Vietnam War was harder on her than my father because she was home in Lincoln, Nebraska, with me, her six-month-old daughter, and Mike, her year-and-half-old son, when my father left for his year-long tour. She was a churchgoing woman who prayed every day for my father, but she said that the fear never left her, and it only grew worse after he came home, afraid that he'd have to go back for another tour.

My mother had prayed for me that night and would pray for me throughout the war like she had prayed for my father while he was in Vietnam, and by now she had found her footing. She was absolutely calm, the way I'd always wanted her to be, and suddenly I wanted her to go back to the mother I'd had growing up, worried about her little girl, how she'd get along in the world. She thought of me as a woman now, a woman who had chosen this life, and I didn't want to let on that on that I was frightened, like a child left alone in a big, old house surrounded by dark and lonely woods.

After I got off the phone, Moshe and Sarah soon went back to bed. No hugs or comforting words. They seemed unmoved, as if they'd lived on an active fault line their whole lives. This was just one more quake. Aviv and I stayed up and watched the news until it was over. Afterwards, a comedian came on and told jokes like this: "I don't know why everyone is worried. Saddam Hussein is going to send three bombs. One will fall in the desert. One will fall in the sea. And the other will fall on my house." We laughed at all the jokes, and when the comedy shows were over, we turned off the television and sat silently for a long while. I wanted to tell Aviv that I'd prayed like my father had as a young soldier in Vietnam, that I'd turned to the all-good God I'd learned about in the Christian Science Sunday school, but I knew that it wouldn't sit well with Aviv. He blamed religion for much of the conflict in the world.

"Do you ever think that maybe, just maybe, there is a God?" I said.

"No," he said, firmly. "I do not believe."

"You never question?"

Aviv cocked his head to the side and looked away from me. "If you grow up in America, it is easy to believe."

"No, it's not."

After a long silence, Aviv said, "If there is a God, He must hate the Jews." He recoiled, like a snail winding into a shell, hands hiding his face drenched in tears. Underneath trembling palms, he breathed, "I have no use for such a God."

The war was a blow to Aviv, a soldier trained to fight rather than sit defenselessly in a sealed room—a gas chamber, to us—hoping that our masks would save us, never knowing if they would be enough, stealing my fiancé's dignity and dreams and manhood. We were vulnerable, like my father's friend in Vietnam. Joe was a commissioned officer stationed at the army post-exchange in Saigon, selling consumer goods to soldiers, when his base was attacked during the Tet Offensive. The Viet Cong overran the base, and he was so traumatized that he broke down and went home early. Joe was a chemical engineer, football star, and level-headed family man like my father, but my father, who saw intense combat in the central highlands and central coast of Vietnam, had a gun and the big guns in the battery to protect him, while this man felt defenseless—like Aviv and I did during the Gulf War. But unlike my father's friend, we were already home.

10
Not a Good Soldier

After another nighttime bombing, Aviv and I went for a walk up the main road, stopping at a café, closed since the war began. We looked through the window at the pastry case. Empty. Almost everything had closed, restaurants and cafés, theaters and malls, schools and universities, small shops and big businesses. Supermarkets and hardware stores stayed open, but shelves were mostly bare where plastic tarps, masking tape, bottled water, canned food, and batteries had been. Aviv already had stocked the sealed room with bottled water, instant soup, and tape, so we stayed at home, day after day.

"Why don't your parents ever ask if I'm okay?"

"It would be an insult," Aviv said.

"An insult?"

"Fear is a weakness."

"We've just been bombed."

"For my parents, this is nothing," Aviv said.

"They aren't afraid?"

"They are used to war."

"How do you get used to war?"

"Live in it all your life."

I shook my head and sobbed. "I can't."

Aviv pulled me to him. "We don't live here. We go to America."

I buried my damp cheek into his chest. "I'm not a good soldier."

Aviv lifted my chin. "I heard my mother talking on the phone to her sister. She was saying how I play a trick on them by bringing you here. They see how nice you are and how brave. My mother thinks you are very, very brave."

My body shivered, the way it did at swim meets as a girl, on those dark rainy days that turned my lips blue. "I'm not a good soldier. Not at all."

A siren went off, and we were out without our gas masks for the first time since the war began. Aviv spun around. "Come on," he said. We sprinted for several blocks. Then he stopped.

"Listen."

"What?"

"It's flat."

We keeled over in laughter. So on edge, we hadn't noticed that the siren sounded the monotone all-clear signal instead of the rise-and-fall warning call to the sealed room.

Sirens would blare all over the country every time Iraq hurled a missile at Israel, sending us to the sealed room over and over during that long, lonely winter, often waking us in the middle of the night. Moshe and Sarah had become remote, like they had put on a coat of invisible armor, while Aviv had become uncharacteristically angry. "I feel like a sitting duck," he would say, again and again. And

I had become overwhelmingly frightened, like an abandoned child, despite Aviv's near constant companionship. I hadn't expected it. Not at all.

I'd always told myself that I was tough. Tough enough to get through anything, Argentina and its army tanks, Peru and its Shining Path guerrillas, the West Bank and its stone-throwing children, a burning fiery furnace. I sought out that kind of trouble and wrote about it for the op-ed page of the *Advocate*—a daily newspaper in Stamford, Connecticut—for almost two years now. Travel essays and political features about fragile democracies in Argentina and Peru, a bloodless revolution on Lake Titicaca, the intifada, and now the Gulf War.

The world was wide and open, and I had a place to write about it. That was all the fuel I needed to brave a war. Or so I thought. For the first time, I felt like I was in the fiery furnace and it was, in fact, burning. It had sunk in, finally, that one of the Scuds could burst on our apartment, hit the refineries and burn up the coast, unleash mustard gas, nerve gas, or some other kind of chemical or biological agent. No matter. The thing is I knew that I could die. That was enough. Plenty.

I had a Hebrew lesson with Moshe. I'd memorized the alphabet. But there was no praise. Moshe pushed ahead to nouns, verbs, short sentences. I remained serious, a perfect mirror of my teacher, who only spoke Hebrew to me. I wondered how a man who spoke so many languages could not try to find one in common with me. Sarah and I had found Spanish, and later practiced English. But Moshe did not try. He seemed to be playing hardball with me until I learned Hebrew.

We worked for several hours until Sarah told us to break. I told her I was going out for a short walk. I tumbled down the stairs to the kiosk next to Aviv's apartment building. Inside the tiny shop, I scanned the cigarettes.

"Camels," I told the clerk.

He slapped the pack down on the counter with a pack of matches. I paid and hustled back to Aviv's, past the cactus garden and the basement bomb shelter to the backyard of the building. I leaned against the stucco wall, picking at the cellophane wrapper, pulling out a cigarette, lighting up, and inhaling bitter tobacco. I had smoked back in New York once, too, when I'd gone to my roommate's new place on the Upper East Side of Manhattan to tell her that Aviv's sister didn't approve of our plans to marry.

Jeanne's father was an Irish Catholic, and her mother was a Jewish atheist who never minded that her daughters went to church.

"Did anyone disapprove of their marriage?" I asked.

"No, my mother's parents were happy. My father was the first conservative guy she had ever dated."

I laughed, but Jeanne could see how stressed I was during those last months without Aviv, as the troop buildup in the Middle East would soon turn into a full-blown war.

"You need this," she said.

I hadn't smoked since the fourth grade, when my baby-sitter gave me a half-finished pack of Marlboros. I brought them to the private Christian Science school I attended and smoked with my friend Geralyn behind a fieldstone wall during recess. I smoked to be cool back then, but now I needed a hit of calm.

11
Nadav

Aviv and Nadav had been friends since early high school, when they studied all night for a computer exam while listening to Coleman Hawkins. The both loved jazz, computers, and basketball. Nadav lived down the street in a ranch house, and Aviv and I went to visit on Martin Luther King's birthday, five days into the Gulf War. Nadav came to the door and smiled, his blue eyes narrowing into slits like mine.

"Come in," he said.

We went to the living room, where a Persian rug covered most of the floor.

"What a beautiful rug," I said.

"My father's family brought it from Austria before Hitler came to town," he said.

Nadav and Aviv used to joke that the Germans were no worse than anyone else. They were just more "efficient."

Aviv walked over to the stereo. "Let's play some of the old guys for her."

"Oscar Peterson?" Nadav said.

Aviv nodded his head and put on Oscar Peterson.

Aviv and Nadav played basketball near the agricultural fields, and sometimes I played too. But they had played on their high school team and were so good that I couldn't keep up. Usually, I'd watch on the sidelines, the way I had in New York when Aviv played pickup games. Aviv and Nadav would play for hours, and I'd often read a book, or go for a run during their games. Afterwards, we'd shower and go for a movie at the Kiryon Mall.

Aviv didn't tell Nadav for more than a month that we were getting married. He worried that Nadav would not approve. When he finally did, Nadav got angry. Not because I wasn't Israeli, not because we were moving to New York, but because Aviv had waited so long to tell him.

12
Housebound

Moshe worked long days at the computer in the sealed room, writing the story of the teenage Zionist imprisoned in the Gulag during World War II and the man who helped smuggle Jews to Palestine after the war. Moshe didn't speak to me or Aviv or Sarah when he worked. He focused like a laser, the way professors did at Penn. Most of them made it clear through their cold stares that they were not there to nurture undergraduates. They were there to write brilliant books. Sarah kept to herself, too. She would spend her days in an alcove off the living room, knitting sweaters for her granddaughter, Nirit. She sat in a rocking chair in a far corner, and often I wouldn't see her all day, apart from lunch. Aviv and I spent our days in Moshe's library, housebound while the university was closed. I read books and the English-language daily, the *Jerusalem Post*, while Aviv read the Hebrew papers *Ha'aretz*, *Ma'ariv*, and *Yedioth Aharonot* and studied for exams. We whispered as if we were in the law school library during final exams.

Moshe, Sarah, and Aviv divided their duties, methodically, like kibbutz members. Aviv handled all electronics—computers, stereos, radios, televisions, VCRs. Moshe handled evening meals—soup and sandwiches mostly. And Sarah did laundry, cleaned, and cooked big meals at lunchtime. She'd cook everything from matzo brei to cholent. Aviv wouldn't touch the meals with meat. He'd pick at the salad and vegetables and snack on apples, cottage cheese, and instant soup. Sarah didn't scold him about it anymore, but she didn't fix him special meals. I ate everything that she cooked, and Sarah would smile and say, "Look, she even eats the cholent." Afterwards, I'd help Sarah clear the table and wash the dishes. We didn't talk much, but I liked being with her. She reminded me of my father's mother, a hard-working woman who never stopped moving. She'd cook and wash and clean all day until it was time for bed. It comforted me.

Moshe made egg salad sandwiches for dinner. He brought them to Aviv and me while we sat in front of the television watching *thirtysomething*. I liked Hope and Michael, who represented the possibilities of an interfaith marriage, even when it was hard. Like the time that Michael went to his rabbi because he felt lost. He was the only link to Judaism, and he wondered how he would integrate his identity into his marriage, and how he would teach his children about who he was. Later, when Aviv and I went back to New York, Aviv would face the same trouble. He had always relied on his family, and more so his country, to provide a sense of identity and tradition. He learned Bible stories in school and took them as Jewish folklore, going back to Abraham and Sarah and Isaac—Yitzhak.

"Do you know why Sarah names him Yitzhak?" Aviv said.

"I don't know," I said.

Aviv smiled. "Sarah names him Yitzhak because it comes from the Hebrew word that means 'to laugh.' She laughed because she gave birth to him in her old age."

Israelis celebrated Jewish holidays as a nation, fasting on Yom Kippur, celebrating the new year on Rosh Hashanah, lighting menorahs on Hanukkah, dressing in costumes on Purim, eating matzo on Passover, planting trees on Tu Bishvat. I didn't have that sort of attachment to Christian Science, a religion without any rituals apart from the daily study of the Bible and *Science and Health*. And nobody passed down any traditions from the English, Scots Irish, and Germans, on my mother's side, or the Danes, Norwegians, and Swiss Germans, on my father's. My father's father, a first-generation American who grew up in a Danish-speaking household, wouldn't even acknowledge that he could understand or speak Danish. He wanted to be American, and like so many in America, he left the old world behind.

13
Cappuccino, Cheesecake, and Gas Masks

Aviv drove his father's stick-shift Renault to the University of Haifa, a skyscraper on Mount Carmel, once schools reopened. And I tagged along, buying espresso in the courtyard before class, knowing I wouldn't understand a word. Students slung gas mask kits over their shoulders as they walked through the hallways. Some spoke Arabic. Aviv said that they were Israeli Arabs, most of them living in Haifa. I hadn't expected such an easy flow, especially during the intifada and now the Gulf War. But Haifa has a mosaic of Baha'is, Muslims, Ahmadis, Christians, and Druze—who serve in the Israeli military—and Aviv said that Arabs and Jews tended to get along better in Haifa than other parts of Israel, like Jerusalem and Tel Aviv, where nearby Jewish settlements in the West Bank caused constant friction. But Haifa's history was not without trouble. During the 1948 Arab-Israeli War, Palestinians fled homes in Haifa and elsewhere, and some refugees and their descendants want the right to return. That has continued to be a sticking point in the Arab-Israeli peace negotiations.

Aviv felt behind because of the time he had spent in the Israeli military and took extra courses to finish and move on to graduate school. He wanted to study the relationship between religion and self-esteem. He thought that people were compelled to "go by the book" because of low self-esteem. What he later found surprised him. His research indicated that those on a quest for answers tend to have high self-worth, while those who worship for social benefits tend to have low. But his findings were inconclusive when it came to fundamentalists. Some had high self-worth, others low. The research softened him, not enough to send his children to church or temple, but enough to respect those who did.

Aviv's professor scrawled statistics formulas on the board. He taught in Hebrew like most of Aviv's professors. He didn't notice me. We were in the last row of stadium seating for hundreds of students. A pretty student in the row ahead of us turned around.

She looked at Aviv. "Is that your sister?"

"My girlfriend," he said.

"Is she a student?"

"No," Aviv said.

She shrugged. "How boring."

I blushed.

Aviv's sociology professor, Zvi Sobel, was American and taught in English. It was Aviv's favorite class. He let me sit in with Aviv, even though it was a small workshop with only a dozen students. Aviv took notes, and I listened. He was a tall man with glasses and the girth of a football player. He had written a book, *Migrants from the Promised Land*, exploring Jewish emigration from Israel during the early 1980s. Professor Sobel found that most were pushed to leave by the constant conflict in the country and pulled by opportunities abroad, particularly in the United States, where most would go. But leaving was taboo, and Aviv knew it. Moving to New York with me went against everything that he had been taught by his family and his country. He used to say, "If everyone does like me, there will be no country." The peer pressure to stay was intense.

Moshe went on a rant about an Israeli actress living in New York. He was furious that she wasn't in Israel during the war. "She should be decent enough to show her face," Moshe said, pounding his fist on the table.

Aviv defended her. "Why, Aba, why must she come for a war?"

"Because she is Israeli."

I hadn't understood, but Aviv explained what his father had said.

During the Gulf War, tens of thousands of Israelis fled places that were frequent targets, like Ramat Gan. Some flew out of the country, and others stayed with relatives and friends or rented hotels in places where missiles had not fallen, safer places like Jerusalem, Beersheva, and Eilat. The mayor of Tel Aviv, Shlomo Lahat, criticized those who left the city while it was under fire. Aviv's sister Ofra was not one of them. She and her husband and baby girl stayed in Ramat Gan throughout the war, even though it took many, many hits. But Revital remained in London, still working for the Israeli government. She didn't come home until the war was over, and Moshe never mentioned her absence. Maybe he would have overlooked Aviv's absence, too, if we had been in New York during the Gulf War. But Aviv and I were there, and I was relieved. Moshe could not think of us as traitors, at least for this war.

After school, Aviv and I went for cheesecake and cappuccino at a café in Haifa. It was the first time we had gone on a date since the air raids began. It surprised me to see so many people driving around, parking their cars, strolling through Haifa with their gas masks kits banging their hips. Newspapers said that Israelis had begun to sell colorful nylon and canvas covers for the kits, and children decorated theirs with Magic Markers. But the only kits I saw were drab brown cardboard.

"I can't believe how many people are out," I said.

"What, you expect everyone to stay home until the war is over?" Aviv stared at his cheesecake, took a bite, didn't look up. It wasn't like him. In New York, he would have taken my hand, caressed it, leaned forward, and given me a kiss.

14
Sitting Ducks

I turned on the computer in Moshe's study and began to write about the Gulf War, wondering how long Israel would keep its promise to stay out of the war, now that Scuds were landing on us, night after night. I faxed the story to my editor and called to see that he had received it. He had, but he hoped that I could revise it, focusing on the mood. So I interviewed an Israeli psychologist, who worked for the mental health hotline set up during the war. She said that adolescent girls called the most, complaining about vomiting and rapid heart rates, while mothers of young children called to sort through feelings of helplessness. "People feel like sitting ducks," she said. "They are angry that they cannot live their normal lives." This was the first large-scale attack on Israeli civilians, and seniors, like Moshe and Sarah, handled it best. "This is nothing new for them," said a social worker in Haifa. "All their lives they have been in war."

Israeli television showed Palestinians cheering in the

West Bank as the first Scuds came in, but that didn't mean they didn't worry, too. A Palestinian man told a reporter, "Saddam's bombs can't tell the difference between Arabs and Jews." He was right. The inaccurate Scuds would fall in the West Bank as well as the desert and the sea. The story ended like this: "While Israelis have started to appear in cafés, shopping malls, and city streets again, they do so with gas mask slung over their shoulders. And every time a noise resembles a siren or bomb, Israelis skip a heartbeat, relieved when it turns out to be just an engine revving or a door slamming." I was one of those people.

I wrote in my Sierra Club calendar every day from the day I landed in Israel through my seven months there, noting the nights we were bombed, where the bombs landed, how many were intercepted. Supposedly. The coalition had urged Israel to stay out of the war and sent Patriot missiles to intercept incoming Scuds. During the war, the coalition gave the Patriot a 96 percent success rate, claiming an intercept every time a Patriot exploded near a Scud. But later it came out that Scuds would break apart on reentry to the atmosphere, and the Patriot would engage part of the missile, while the warhead would travel on and explode anyway.

After the war, the U.S. Army would downgrade the Patriot's success rate in Israel to 40 percent, meaning probable success for about seven out of the seventeen attempted interceptions in Haifa and Tel Aviv—where Patriot missiles were installed after twelve Scuds struck those cities in the first two attacks on Israel—with the army's highest confidence rating given to fewer than three. At the same time, several Patriots struck ground and exploded without engaging any Scuds, and those that burst in the air added to the falling debris. Experts would point out, too, that blowing up Scuds over cities would spread chemical and biological toxins more effectively than a ground explosion.

The Israelis were less confident in the Patriot all along. After each Scud attack the Israeli military investigated the site of impact, and it was clear that the Patriot was not nearly as effective as the coalition claimed. The news was not shared with the public until after the war, when Israeli defense minister Moshe Arens would tell PBS's *Frontline* that initially he thought the Patriot had intercepted maybe 20 percent of the Scuds, but later he concluded that the Patriot probably failed to intercept a single Scud. At the time, however, I thought it was working and kept track of the air raids, interceptions, and everyday life in my calendar. It was a spare diary of that winter, 1991.

January 15. United Nations deadline to withdraw from Kuwait.
January 16. Quiet night.
January 17. Coalition bombs Baghdad. Gulf War begins.
January 18. First air raid at 2:20 a.m. Haifa, Tel Aviv hit. Talk to Mom.
January 19. Tel Aviv hit. Early morning attack.
January 20. Quiet night.
January 21. Martin Luther King's birthday. Visit Nadav. Quiet night.
January 22. Early morning air raid on Tel Aviv.
January 23. Scud fired at Haifa. Patriot engages.

January 24. Aviv goes back to school. Brings gas mask. Quiet night.

January 25. Haifa and Tel Aviv targeted. Some intercepted.

January 26. Haifa and Tel Aviv targets intercepted!

January 27. Quiet night.

January 28. Hebrew class with Moshe. Send story to *Advocate*. West Bank hit.

January 29. Mom calls. Quiet night. Read Harold Saunders's *The Other Walls*.

January 30. Read Chaim Potok's *The Promise*. Story runs about mood, grim. Quiet night.

January 31. Aviv takes linear algebra exam. Housebound three days. West Bank hit.

February 1. Quiet night.

February 2. West Bank again. Visit Ofra's in-laws.

February 3. West Bank again.

February 4. Aviv has statistics exam. Hard. Quiet night.

February 5. Go out for cheesecake. Bring gas mask. Quiet night.

February 6. Jog five miles. Letter from Mom. Quiet night.

February 7. Sit on bench, read paper, smoke. Nervous. Quiet night.

February 8. Aviv tutors boy whose father is in America. Quiet night.

February 9. Thirty-minute run, read Simone de Beauvior's *The Prime of Life*. Tel Aviv hit.

February 10. Aviv takes calculus exam. Talk to Mom. Visit Nadav. Quiet night.

February 11. Scud fired at Tel Aviv.

February 12. Mall, movies, beach. Early morning attack on Tel Aviv.

February 13. Quiet night.

February 14. Valentine's Day. Aviv gives me card, book *The Seed of Abraham*. Quiet.

The war went on like that, a mix of air raids and everyday life, gas masks and sealed rooms, cheesecake and Valentine's Day cards. My gut became a pit of nerves, so deep that I'd smoke and run and write and talk. And read and read and read. Book after book after book. History books, sociology books, novels, memoirs, short stories, anything to keep me too busy to think too hard about Scuds and oil refineries and chemical warfare. I read books by Raphael Patai, Barnet Litvinoff, Wolf Blitzer, Jacobo Timerman, George Orwell, Franz Kafka, Gabriel García Márquez, Julio Cortázar, Jerome K. Jerome, Ernest Hemingway. Twenty-three books in seven months, through the war and afterwards. They steadied me, kept me going those long afternoons when Aviv was away at school and those long winter nights waiting for the air-raid siren to wail. I listed them all in the back of the calendar, marking time, seeking order. There was none.

15

The Promise

We drove in silence along the Mediterranean, alfalfa fields, a vast blanket of purple blooms growing beside the coastal highway. Aviv slumped in the driver's seat, cheeks hollowed by war. Scuds had fallen on Israel, over and over for a month now, and I wondered if he'd ever recover. Aviv was so proud of his country, its beauty and its fierceness, and it had become an inhospitable place, crushing his dreams of peace.

"Are we going to be happy again like we were in the beginning?" I broke our silence.

He stared ahead at the road. "We will be happy, I promise," he said.

Aviv and I pulled into the kibbutz below Mount Carmel on the edge of the Jezreel Valley—the valley that "God sows"—fertile farmland sprouting avocados, almonds, persimmons, peaches, plums, kiwis, cotton, sunflowers, barley, corn, and wheat. Three million years ago, the valley connected the Mediterranean to the Dead Sea. I would work on the kibbutz and study Hebrew as part of an ulpan, an Israeli government program that provides Hebrew lessons and housing to new immigrants. I wasn't exactly an immigrant, but I had written a heartfelt letter about wanting to study Hebrew and learn about Aviv's country before we married, and sent it in with my application to the ulpan back in New York. The man in the New York office had told me that my chances of getting into the program were slim, especially now that so many immigrants were coming to Israel, some from Ethiopia as part of Operation Solomon but most from the Soviet Union as it was about to collapse. More than fourteen thousand Jews from the Soviet Union and seventeen hundred from Ethiopia would arrive in January and February despite the war, and nearly a million Jewish immigrants, including seven hundred thousand from the former Soviet Union and forty thousand from Ethiopia, would arrive during the 1990s, the government promising housing and Hebrew lessons to everyone making aliyah. And for some Ethiopians Hebrew would be their first written language.

Aviv parked in front of a ranch-style building that looked like my elementary school, where I'd jumped off the roof into a pile of leaves.

"Ready?" Aviv said.

"Ready," I said.

Aviv and I reached for the door openers, looking at each other like cliff divers about to take a simultaneous plunge. I nodded, and we opened. I stepped into a mild February day, sunny and springlike. A sweater and jeans was enough, even though I chilled easily, the way runners do after workouts.

"So you think it's that way?" I pointed to a paved path bordered by pines. Needles scattered on the path, their fragrance evidence of last night's rain. The kibbutz smelled of pine.

"I think that must be the way," he said.

The path opened into a grassy compound, cabins on one side and homes on the other. The homes were duplexes with brick facades and Renaults like Moshe's parked out front. The milky-gray cabins reminded me of those at summer camp in the Poconos. Aviv said that the cabins were for the volunteers, like me, and the homes were for members of the kibbutz.

Aviv pointed to a white clapboard house beyond the homes and cabins. "This building must be the office," he said.

"Strange that there are no people out," I said.

"It's Saturday. The day of rest on the kibbutz."

"Come on, let's get this over with." I went in.

"You are here for the ulpan?" I heard a woman call from the adjoining room.

"Yes."

"Come in here," she called out. It was Migdala, the director of the ulpan. She looked up from the manila folder in the center of her desk, as if she had just graded my exam. From her stern look, I could tell that I had done poorly.

"It says here that you are not Jewish."

"I'm not, but—" I stopped.

Eyes down, focused on my worn-out running shoes, I wanted to tell her about the book I'd just read, *The Seed of Abraham*, about how Arabs and Jews are brothers because they're both descendants of Abraham, who fathered Ishmael and Isaac. That book got me thinking about how Jesus was a Jew, only he had another take on things. And how scholars compare the Hindu Upanishads to Jesus' teachings in the New Testament. Maybe there are so many religions in the world because of man's need to see individually, the way different students thrive under different teaching methods. Could there be such a difference between gentile and Jew, observant and atheist, Muslim and Christian, Hindu and Buddhist? Aren't we all in this life together, ultimately? Brothers and sisters all?

"She was accepted in New York," Aviv said. He leaned his palms on the desk as if looking over the papers, to show her some note that indicated that the officials had not let me in by mistake, that they knew I wasn't Jewish but wanted to give me the chance anyway to be part of the ulpan, to learn Hebrew and work on the kibbutz and taste Israel, even if I didn't decide to convert and live there always.

"Fine," she said, slapping the creamy folder together. Case closed.

I balled up a gray V-neck, khakis, and flannel shirt. Aviv picked up combat boots, tied the laces, slung them over his shoulder, and pushed through the screen door. His shoulders slumped, chin bowed into chest. He shuffled his chocolate suede boots along the asphalt, scuffing his crepe soles like a kid sick of the shopping mall. He stopped at my cabin to drop off the clothes and my backpack. I wanted him to say something, reassure me that everything would be fine on the kibbutz, that we'd make it through the rest of the war and get back to New York, where we had always been happy. The cavity of his cheeks sunk in deep, and plum rings stained his eyes. And he was silent.

"Come, we go for coffee," he said. He had an exam that afternoon and had to get going.

We backtracked along the path that led to the kibbutz office. Pine trees rocked in the breeze.

"We can go in there for a coffee." Aviv pointed to the brick building that reminded me of my elementary school. Inside, it looked like a lunchroom. Big tables lined up in rows. The cafeteria was to the side. The bins were empty. We had come too late for lunch and too early for dinner. Aviv spotted packets of Nescafé and the hot water spout. He prepared two coffees in orange plastic cups, the same orange plastic as the furniture in my cabin.

"Come, we sit at a table." Aviv carried the cups to a table near the window. It overlooked a lawn big as a football field. Another gray-white farmhouse like the kibbutz office was at the opposite end. "You are okay?" Aviv asked.

My eyes welled with tears as Aviv reached across the table and held my hand. "I'm going to miss you," I said.

"I want you to call me," he said as he stroked the back of my hand with his thumb. "Promise me that you will call whenever you need to talk."

"I can't promise you that," I said.

"But there, you see, there is a phone." He pointed to a pay phone in the foyer.

"That's not the problem."

He stopped stroking my hand.

"I'd be on the phone all the time, and they'd have to kick me out of the ulpan."

We walked to the silver-gray Renault borrowed from his

father. "You are going to be my good soldier here. Everybody is going to love you, even that Migdala when she sees how good you are working and how fast you are learning Hebrew. Even from what my father teaches you in one month you already are making small conversation."

Aviv pulled me to him as he leaned against the driver's side door. I nestled my cheek into the cavity between neck and shoulder and closed my eyes. The memory of his warmth would get me through that first week. It would have to.

"I'm going to miss you so much," I said into his shoulder.

He stroked my hair, patting my head and fanning his hand down the nape of my neck, slowing moving down to the middle of my back.

Aviv got into the car and rolled down the window.

"Call me, whatever time doesn't matter. You understand?"

"I do."

Aviv pulled out of the lot toward the main road and the alfalfa fields, where we had driven in silence, past blankets of purple blooms.

16
Lucie

I had a good feeling about my roommate, Lucie. She was a petite brunette with a mane of brown curls and a lovely, singsongy voice. She reminded me of the teenage daughter of the family that hosted me in France, as part of a Penn study abroad program in Compiègne. My French "mother" was a tour guide at the Chateau de Compiègne, and deep in the forest where royalty used to hunt is a replica of the car where Germany signed the armistice ending World War I; where France signed a truce with Hitler during World War II; and where Nazis and collaborators held Jews, Gypsies, immigrants, homosexuals, resistance fighters, and political prisoners before deporting them in cattle cars to concentration camps in Germany and Austria and Poland—Auschwitz, Buchenwald, Mauthausen, Ravensbrück. I wondered if the town hoped to make amends for its past by hosting students from Penn, an Ivy League university that has always had many Jewish students. I would never ask.

Lucie and I shared a small room with two single beds, two desks, an armoire, and a side table with a hot pot to make coffee and tea. The chairs, cups, and saucers were tangerine plastic.

"So what brings you here in the middle of the war?" I asked. I imagined she was wondering the same about me.

Lucie stuffed a pair of black-and-white, vertical-striped leggings into the armoire. She turned toward me, her skin alabaster, as if all her blood had been siphoned.

"My mother sends me," she said.

"During a war?"

"Yes, she arranges everything."

"Why?"

Lucie had failed her baccalaureate, and her mother didn't approve of her boyfriend, Jean Pierre. A black Catholic from Martinique. Lucie's mother was old-world French Moroccan, and she wanted Lucie go to Israel to get in touch with her Jewish roots.

"And you, why do you come here now?"

"I'm engaged to an Israeli."

"Super," she said it like the daughter of my French family, su-*pear*. She picked up her knees and pressed them to her chest, locking her palms over her shins. "I am sad from missing my boyfriend." She tapped her red-and-white pack of Marlboros on the side table, pulled out a cigarette, and offered the pack to me. "You like one?"

"Why not," I said, and took one from the pack.

Lucie lit her cigarette and passed her burning end to me. I held it up to mine and inhaled until the tobacco turned electric orange and handed it back. I leaned against the wall and inhaled. Lucie held her cigarette, leaned forward, and pressed her legs into a split.

116

"So, are you a gymnast?"

"A dancer."

Of course, a dancer. Dancers always smoke. I knew that. I lived near Lincoln Center in Manhattan. Ballet dancers pranced along Broadway in leggings like Lucie's puffing on cigarettes pressed delicately between forefingers.

I looked out the window at the pines.

"Me, I'm a runner," I said, mindlessly taking a drag from my cigarette. "I want to do a marathon someday." It struck me how absurd it was that I was smoking. Me, the runner, smoking. I didn't think of it as a habit, yet. I had only been smoking for a few months and only a few cigarettes now and then. I never imagined that I would return to New York addicted to those few. But soon enough, I would become a pack-a-day smoker, until I finally quit four years later.

17
A Lonely Trip

Inside the cafeteria, the lights were on. The sky turned gray and was darkening fast. I heard dishes clanging in the kitchen, and I smelled cafeteria food—beef stew, boiled carrots, peas, and potatoes.

"Are you hungry?"

"No, I only want a coffee."

"Dancers don't eat?"

She shrugged.

"Go, sit, and I'll bring you coffee."

"Two spoons of sugar."

Lucie felt like my little sister, and I'd always felt more like a mother than sister to Cindy, aware that I was supposed to protect her and wrecked when I failed. Like the time she got nailed in the eye with a baseball, a clean line right from the bat to her eye as she squatted on second base. And like the time she visited me at Penn and I left her alone at a frat party so I could dance with my boyfriend. She was as tall as I was and bustier, so I forgot she was only thirteen and didn't know how to manage at a college keg party even for one dance.

I emptied Nescafé packets into the tangerine cups, filled them with hot water, and added milk and sugar. Then I got a plate of beef stew for myself.

"Here you go," I said.

She sipped her coffee.

A guy holding an orange tray of food headed toward us. I was struck by his good looks. He had broad shoulders, like a swimmer's, blue eyes, and dark curls.

He held his dinner tray. "Mind if I sit with you?"

"You sit with us, of course," Lucie said.

Jeremy told us he was British, that he'd already been on another kibbutz for six months, and that he was bored out of his mind. Later, I would suspect that he was MI6, a British spy.

That night, I unpacked and stuffed my cardboard box—complete with gas mask, confectionery sugar-like antidote, and atropine needle—under the bed. I realized I'd forgotten to find out about the shelter. Were we supposed to put tarps over the window and seal our cabins? I hoped for a quiet, bomb-free night. I sat down on my bed, propped up my pillow against the wall, and read a letter from my father. He talked about war, how hard it is, how he was thinking of me. He had written letters every day while he was in Vietnam, a thick volume I would not read until I was a grown woman who knew about war herself. At night, he'd look up at the abundance of stars and think of my mother and brother and me, overcome by his deep longing for home. By now, I understood that war wasn't a big adventure, like my grandfather had made it seem. It was a lonely trip that you hoped would soon end.

18
Hebrew Lessons

My alarm clock went off. Lucie didn't stir. Her mass of brown curls sprawled on the pillow, and her tiny body bent into a fetal position facing the opposite wall. I let her sleep while I went to the showers behind our cabin. The sun was out, piercing through the clear sky into my skin. I could feel my skin parch. I thought of Aviv's mother, how she'd noticed the lines. "You come here with perfect skin. What happens to you?" I wanted to say, "Are you kidding? There's a war on. These are worry lines." Instead, I promised her that I'd use more face cream.

I put on my flannel shirt, khakis, and combat boots.

Lucie had not moved from her fetal crunch. I patted her on the shoulder.

"Time to get up."

She moaned and rolled onto her back. "Café," she said.

"I don't think there's time."

Lucie sat up and rubbed her eyes and glided to the

armoire. She put on her leggings, sailor shirt, and black-and-white Adidas.

"Not your work clothes?"

She scrunched up her nose. "So ugly," she said.

She told me that she would be working in the kibbutz day-care center. She didn't need to wear work clothes like mine.

"We better go," I said.

Lucie and I walked to the kibbutz office. Migdala sat at her desk, flipping through manila folders as more volunteers arrived. The office was jammed with volunteers. They were all speaking in Russian, wearing work clothes like mine. Lucie was the only one who was not dressed for farm or factory work. We went back out to the porch and saw Jeremy on his way up to the office. His cabin was among a cluster by the cow pen. He wore a flannel shirt and khakis, almost the same outfit as mine, but instead of combat boots, he wore knee-high rubber boots spattered with mud.

"Morning," he said.

"*Bonjour*," Lucie said.

I smiled.

Lucie, Jeremy, and I squeezed into the waiting room. The din of Russian chatter kept us quiet in the corner. The teacher kept calling out names, testing each volunteer in an adjoining room. Finally, I heard mine.

Inside, it looked like an elementary school classroom. A blackboard, small wooden desks for students, and a big steel one for the teacher, Hannah.

"Shalom," she said.

"Shalom," I said.

She wanted to test my Hebrew and asked me to write the alphabet, which I did perfectly. Moshe had drilled me daily for a month, and I had it down pat. Then she asked me to write a few words in Hebrew, and I jotted them quickly.

"*Nachon*," she said. Correct.

"*At medaberet Ivrit?*" Do you speak Hebrew?

"*Ken, ketsat.*" Yes, a little.

We had a short, simple conversation in Hebrew, and when it was over, she smiled as if I would be her star pupil and told me that I'd be in the advanced class. How odd. Did she realize I was not Jewish, that I'd only picked up what I knew over the last month from Aviv's father? That I'd never been to Hebrew school?

"Did you pass?" Jeremy asked as he edged by me on my way out of the classroom.

"Think so."

Volunteers gathered on the porch after the Hebrew test. Later, I learned that there were thirty volunteers in the ulpan. Lucie, Jeremy, and I were among the handful of Westerners.

Lucie and Jeremy came out to the porch. "See that," he said.

He pointed to a bone-colored building on the other side of the path, mostly hidden behind thick pines. It was the air-raid shelter. I hadn't noticed it, despite passing it at least half a dozen times.

Lucie stared wide-eyed at the shelter.

"Do they seal it?" I asked.

"Why bother? Saddam Hussein won't use chemical weapons."

"But how do you know he won't?"

He shrugged.

I went inside the classroom, sat next to a man with dark curly hair and a thick mustache.

"America?" the man said.

"Yes," I said.

"Lev, from Ukraine. Where are your friends?"

"They're in the beginners' class."

"And you, who are not Jewish, are speaking better?"

"Is it that obvious?"

"To me, yes." He scanned my face with his big blue eyes, inspecting the way my mother did. I never knew how people saw me, exactly. I had a Danish name and hybrid looks. Long chestnut hair, high cheekbones, summertime freckles, and slanted blue eyes that I thought had to do with my Native American roots. I was thirty when my mother found out that it was one of my grandfather's tall tales. We believed him because he looked like a Native American chief, except for his blue eyes. My mother always said that I looked like her mother, the Rockette, but I was sensitive about my looks as the only brunette in a family of blondes, though my mother and sister no longer had the natural blonde hair of their teens.

The teacher stood up and went to the blackboard. She wrote the alphabet and her name, Hannah. Then she asked me to read the alphabet aloud for the class.

"*Alef, bet*," I said, and went on through the whole alphabet.

"*Todah*." Thank you, she said.

Once we finished with the alphabet, Hannah wrote several basic words on the blackboard. She said the word in Russian and then English as she drew an image and spelled out the Hebrew word on the blackboard. She had us each pronounce the words, which were already part of my limited vocabulary. In my turn, I said the words.

"*Nachon*." Right, she said.

Hannah handed out a photocopy to each student. The paper reproduced the images on the blackboard. As homework, we were supposed to write out the Hebrew word to describe each image. Hannah excused the class and reminded us that we had one hour for lunch, then we were to report to work until 6 p.m.

"You go for lunch?" Lev asked.

"Yes, and you?"

"We go eat and then to working."

We walked down toward the cafeteria together. "The bomb shelter." I pointed it out.

"Yes, yes. I know it from my wife. She asks about it."

"Are you worried?"

"No, no, so much worries in Russia, I can't worry more."

"I've been here the whole time. North of Haifa with my fiancé."

"Ah, now I understand you."

I smiled. I liked Lev. He was probably forty, youthful, but fatherly. Kind. We filed into the cafeteria. Boiled string beans, spaghetti and tomato sauce. It looked bland, like hospital food, but I was hungry and filled my plate.

"Lev." I heard a woman call.

"This is my wife, Elana." Lev introduced me and said, "She is the best in our class."

I blushed.

Elana turned to Lev and spoke to him in Russian.

"My wife, she speaks little English."

"That's okay, I want to eat and then run to my room before work anyway."

I found a seat near the window, alone. I looked for Lucie and Jeremy but didn't see them in the crowded lunchroom. How odd so few people were around yesterday. Now it was teeming with people—entering, exiting, cooking, eating, talking, scratching, sitting. I looked out the window at the lawn. Mustard patches marred the grass, burned yellow in the sun. I thought of Aviv, our coffee here yesterday. Could I call him? Then I remembered it was Sunday. He had classes all day and then had to tutor a boy for the scholarship program PERACH, an acronym that means "flower" in Hebrew.

19
Scandinavian Worker

Down at the factories, a man loaded orange plastic trays into boxes. I scanned back and forth, looking for the plastics factory, the place I had to report for work. I asked the man loading trays. He looked up. His face was weathered like a fisherman's, creased and ruddy. He had on bib overalls and a red thermal shirt.

"The last one." He pointed toward the end of the row of milky white cinder block factories.

"*Todah*," I said.

"You're welcome," he said, in English. Hardly an accent.

I walked past the open gates to the factories. Conveyor belts ferried orange plastic meal trays, coffee cups, folding chairs, TV tables. The kibbutz made money off plastics. At the last factory, I rounded the corner looking for the entrance. It didn't have a big, two-car-garage-sized gate like the others, only a home-style wooden door at the base of a stairwell. I went down and pushed in. Black grease coated the concrete floor, like an auto mechanic's garage.

Table saws stood in the middle of the room by waist-high cylindrical bins filled with silver strips. A man walked out of an adjoining room.

"Shalom," he said.

"Shalom," I said.

"Ah, so you are my new worker," he smiled. His eyes were hazel, big and round. He was bronzed and lined like the other factory worker but not as severely. His skin was still mostly smooth, except for the lines around his eyes when he smiled. His short, silver-and-smoke hair was a dense cap. He had on the kibbutz uniform—flannel work shirt, cotton slacks, and black work boots.

"Ya'akov," he said. He spoke so assertively and with warmth that surprised me.

"Karol, from America," I said.

"Welcome, Karol from America," he said. "Come, I show you your work. We are not the plastic factories like our neighbors. Here, we are cutting," Ya'akov said, chopping the back of one hand with his other. "Here, we are making a very important business. You have seen a refrigerator in America I'm sure." He grinned.

I laughed. I liked him already.

"Well, if you can remember what is inside your refrigerator besides your vegetables and your fruits, you will see what we are making here."

I looked at the table saws and the silvery scraps, wide as two fingers and tall as an interior wall—eight, nine, maybe ten feet long. "The lip of the shelves?"

"You are 100 percent correct." He picked up one of the silver strips, and it wobbled. "These guys look like they are going to be tough to cut, but don't be fooled. This is only plastic from our factories. You're cutting these long pieces into three small pieces. Come, I show you how this business works. But first we put on our mask."

Ya'akov went over to a shelf near the back room, which had a table and chairs inside. He picked up two sets of clear goggles, big as snorkeling masks. "You always wear the mask. You understand? A finger you can live without, but your eye, that is something you don't want to lose."

I nodded and reached for my mask.

"Do you talk, Karol from America?"

I laughed. "Yes, even some Hebrew."

"Here you can speak English. I will wait until you feel like speaking to this old man."

I laughed again. I wanted to speak to him, but I was not sure where to begin.

"Come, put on the glasses, and I show you this machine," he said.

I put on my goggles like Ya'akov. He flipped the red switch on the cylindrical base of the saw. The disc began spinning, its teeth bleeding into a smooth round surface as it reached full speed. He fit the long undulating silver strip onto the table and lowered the circular saw until the plastic split off. He tossed the cut strip into the bin next to the base of the saw and slid the uncut portion into place. "We cut 555, 615, and 656 millimeters." He pointed to the ruler embedded on the table. "You like to try?"

"I think I get it."

"Good. Today we are cutting 615 millimeters. You are going to have a piece left at the end. It will be too short for using so you put it in that one." He pointed to another waist-high bin on the other side of the saw. He handed me the strip.

I fit the piece along the table, measuring 615 millimeters from the mouth of the saw. I held the plastic down a few inches from the spot where the blade would sever the plastic. The tail flopped off the other end of the table, and I worried the strip would pop out of place unless I pressed down firmly with my fingers. I lowered the saw slowly, slicing into the plastic. It snapped apart. I tossed the cut piece into the finished pieces bin, slid the uncut portion down the saw.

Ya'akov walked over to a bin full of silver strips almost grazing the ceiling pipes. "You do like this," he said. He grabbed a bundle and tossed them at my feet under the table saw. They clanged like cymbals as they settled into position.

"Good?" he said.

"Good."

Ya'akov went back to the other room, and I fit the rest of the piece I had begun to cut into place: 615 millimeters. I pressed my fingers hard, too hard considering the end barely stuck out past the edge of the table this time. I lowered the saw, training my eyes on the spot it would sever, equally focused on my forefinger and thumb holding the piece in place. I could only imagine how easy it would be to slice a finger in a careless moment. The saw spun as I drew it down and watched it shred the plastic, whisking away silver flecks as it worked through the strip. I threw the finished piece in the bin to my side. Flung the scrap in the other one. Kneeled and got another strip and started over again.

I gave myself orders as I worked: Line it up, press finger

and thumb, lower saw, watch it snap, toss it over, kneel for another. Again. Fit, press, lower, toss, kneel, grab, fit. I found my groove and worked rhythmically, pacing myself the way I do on a long-distance run. Inhale, pump arms, lift thighs, roll heels, exhale, pump, lift, lower, breathe. I listened to the screeching grind of the saw, its piercing whistle as it sliced the plastic, the clanging strips at my boots. The sounds were reliable like the pounding of my pulse and feet, the heavy inhaling and exhaling, on my runs. When I finished the batch below the table saw, I gathered another bunch from the bin near the adjoining room. I peered in. A marbled emerald Formica table took up most of the room. A sink and stove sat below the window. The view was a grassy mound sloping down from the sidewalk. The factory was in the basement.

I couldn't see Ya'akov. For the moment I was working alone. I could have slacked off, but I preferred the work. It relaxed me, kept me from worrying about air raids. As I dumped my second stack of silver strips under the saw, Ya'akov reappeared through the door behind me, the entryway I came through when I arrived. A woman followed and then a man. They came in single file down the steps. The woman had short dark hair and a square, manly jaw. She towered above Ya'akov, as did Dov, whose thick, dark hair was cropped short like a soldier's.

"This is Adira," Ya'akov said, nodding to the woman. "And Dov." He tapped Dov on the shoulder.

"Shalom," Dov said.

"Shalom," Adira said, already walking out of the room.

"Look, she is already working like a professional," Ya'akov said, beaming, to Dov.

Dov and Ya'akov moved to the other machines. I reached down and got my piece and began again, fitting, pressing, lowering, tossing, kneeling. I lost myself in the rhythm, though never losing sight of my fingers and their distance from the blade. I was aware, the way I am running, of every moving part, sensing the muscles and tendons rise and bend, stretch and pound, feeling each movement, ensuring nothing is straining unnaturally. No muscles pulling. No fingers getting cut off. I picked up my pace and got through the second batch more quickly than the first. I was uncertain what pace was normal, so I pushed ahead, finding my own rhythm, forgetting everyone else to focus on my pace, my movement, my task.

Ya'akov tapped me on the shoulder as I tossed a cut piece into the finished pieces bin.

"Karol from America, time to break, have a coffee, sit."

He nudged me toward the kitchen.

"Okay, sure." I was startled by the interruption, but I followed him to the green table.

"Go, make a coffee," he said. "Dov and I are already drinking our cup."

I went over to the stove, next to Adira, who was pouring hot water into an orange plastic cup. Her left forefinger had a blunt edge, sliced clean like the tip of a loaf of bread. She swung around and took a seat at the table with Ya'akov and Dov. I made my Nescafé, trembling as if I'd spent too much in a sprint. I sat down next to Ya'akov. A round tin of butter cookies was on the table.

"Have a biscuit. Two," Ya'akov said. He grabbed a couple and set them down on the table by my cup. He leaned back in his chair, the legs lifting up off the cement floor. Then he rolled back to the table and sipped his coffee.

"I like how the Scandinavians work. Hard," he said as he pounded his fist onto the table and smiled at me. He was a small man but exuded energy far beyond his size.

Ya'akov had to stop me at six. He probably could see I would go on unless he stopped me. I liked it in the factory. It was solitary because of the grinding noise that made small talk difficult. Maybe I should have told them my story during the break. Ya'akov gave me the opportunity, and they were probably curious, even Adira. I bet they wanted to know what this American was doing on an Israeli kibbutz during the Gulf War. It didn't take long to tell Ya'akov that I was getting married to Aviv, but that day I just wanted to work like any other member of the ulpan.

I walked back to the cabin. Lucie wasn't there. Probably with Jeremy. I wanted to call Aviv and tell him all about my first day on the kibbutz—how I got into the advanced Hebrew class and met Lev from Ukraine and had lunch by myself at a table by the windows where we'd had coffee. And how I cut refrigerator shelf lips all afternoon. I was okay. I'd make it. I'd tell him I bet time would fly on the kibbutz, that his semester would be over before we knew it, and we could get back to New York, back to the good times we had before the war. But I knew that he was out, tutoring that little boy whose father had gone to America and sent pictures home, shots of him by his shiny new Pontiac Grand Am.

20
Pampered American

The air-raid siren jolted me awake.

"Lucie," I said.

The room was dark. I could see her on the bed, and I leapt toward her. "Get up, get up, the alarm. We have to run." This time, unlike the morning, she hopped up, dressed in leggings and a sweatshirt. I pulled on the khakis and the flannel shirt I'd worn to work. "Your shoes, the mask, hurry," I said, as I grabbed my boots, gas mask box, and Lucie's hand. Her palm sweat into mine.

"Let's go," I said, tugging her hand.

We bolted to the shelter. It was across the path, opposite our cabin. Inside, Lev, his wife, and children were already there. They had come in their pajamas, bare feet, no masks. Unprepared for chemical warfare, like Moshe and Sarah had been. Where were their masks? Should I give mine up, but to whom? Lev, his wife, his youngest, his oldest, boy, girl?

Lucie sat in an armchair and clawed at her gas mask

container. She pried it open and snatched her mask. She slapped the black rubber to her face, and feathered her tiny fingers across the seal, pulling out tufts of brown curls to make sure the seal was tight. She flopped into the worn-velvet armchair.

I squeezed her shoulder. "You okay?"

She bobbed her head.

Other volunteers, bare-footed and sleepy-eyed, straggled into the concrete bomb shelter. Where was Jeremy? I waited. I didn't know that there was another shelter closer to his cabin where he would take cover. So I worried. We needed to close the door, to seal out nerve gas, toxic chemicals, more at risk in this ground-level shelter. I began to feel that I was the only one who knew, or cared. Lucie and I were the only ones with gas masks. Most had ample flesh exposed. Didn't they know that the bombs might release poison gas and chemicals? Didn't they know bare skin was most vulnerable to contamination? Didn't they care about the children? For God's sake, what about the children? It was like going to battle without a gun. I flipped open my box, grabbed the mask, and slipped it on. Snap. I checked the seal. It was tight. How many times had I done this already? More than a month of air raids, sending us to the sealed room sixteen times that felt like a hundred.

The door was still open. I darted to the entrance, looked out, and didn't see anyone on the way to the shelter. I slammed the steel door shut and inspected the jamb. I ran my finger along it and couldn't feel any draft. It wasn't the right kind of shelter, but it would have to do. Later, I would come to understand that even a sealed room would not provide protection from toxic vapors that would seep into the room after a few hours, unless it had ventilation. But I did not know that then, and I worried about being in this conventional, ground-level shelter that wasn't sealed.

I sat down next to Lucie, on the arm of an over-stuffed chair. There was nothing else to do now, except wait. We were more than a dozen miles from Haifa and should have been out of range. But the Scuds were inaccurate. Some had fallen short of Tel Aviv and landed in the West Bank, as coalition forces hunted mobile launchers and pushed them farther into Iraq. How could we be sure they wouldn't fall here, too? Even if they fell somewhere else, how could we be sure they wouldn't contain chemicals? Toxins could travel miles if the winds were right. That was the problem with this sort of war. We could not be sure of anything.

At Aviv's, we listened to the radio while we huddled in the sealed room. But here there was no radio, only the chatter of sleepy Russians, Ukrainians, and others from the Soviet Union, who stared at Lucie and me. They looked perplexed by our masks. Even Lev eyed me with a raised eyebrow as if surprised that I wore a mask, that I closed the door to the shelter, that I looked so worried. For me, the feelings of fear and isolation intensified with each raid, and I wondered if they would have been so blasé if they had heard explosions like me. Didn't I already have enough to worry about? Couldn't Aviv and I have been like normal couples who fall in love, marry, and worry about ordinary things? Mortgages, children, in-laws. Why did we have to live through a war? And why had Lev and his family and the rest of the volunteers come without masks? Why hadn't they covered their skin? Why did I have to worry about them, too? Why did I have to feel like a hypochondriac, a pampered American, a ridiculous fool, for trying to stay alive?

I was so unprepared.

Lucie looked at me through her black mask, probably wondering how long we'd have to wait. Sometimes we'd waited in the sealed room for more than an hour for the all-clear siren to sound, and by now I was used to the mask, the heat, the pungent rubber, the nausea. But it was new to Lucie, and I knew how the discomfort could intensify to a sensation of suffocation because of the desire to breathe quickly, as quickly as your racing pulse. The siren moaned and shrieked, making my stomach and jaw clench as they did each raid. I listened and waited, trying to pace my breathing, gently rubbing Lucie's shoulder. I couldn't comfort her verbally, but I could at least try to calm her with touch. I didn't hear any explosions, but I wondered if the missiles were hitting Haifa. Ripping off facades, smashing roofs, burning grassy earth bare.

The flat-toned, all-clear siren blared. The air raid was over. We could remove the masks, leave the shelter, return to bed. I lifted my mask and inhaled, closing my eyes and repeating several deep breaths.

"You ready?" I asked Lucie, dazed in the armchair, her mask in her little lap. "Come on, we need to sleep."

"Yes, yes, I come," she said.

I put my arm around Lucie's shoulder, and we walked back to our cabin, masks in our hands.

"Are you okay?" I asked.

"Yes, yes," Lucie said, face down toward the asphalt path. Back in the room I sat down on the bed and watched

Lucie curl into her fetal crunch, face against the wall. I was relieved that she did not want to talk, yet I surprised myself with this. After the other raids, I'd been desperate to be alone with Aviv, without his parents. My need was urgent, to talk and nestle in Aviv's lap, my cheek against his, sobbing. I couldn't risk doing that in front of Moshe and Sarah. Crying in front of them would have convinced them that I'd never be strong enough to live in Israel, that I'd take their boy away to America and never come back. I wanted them to think that I could take it, that I was durable enough, that I could live there, even if it was a full-blown act.

Before dawn, the air-raid siren went off again. I had been at the pay phones in the cafeteria, trying to call Aviv, but could not get through. I called home instead, and my mother comforted me with lines from the 91st Psalm:

He shall cover thee with his feathers, and under his wings shalt thou trust: his truth shall be a shield and buckler.
  Thou shalt not be afraid for the terror by night; nor for the arrow that flieth by day . . . For he shall give his angels charge over thee, to keep thee in all they ways.

"The siren," I said. "It's going off again."
"I love you," she said.
I ran to the room, got Lucie and our gas masks, and hurried to the bomb shelter. Hardly anyone else bothered to come.

I woke after a few hours of sleep. It was nearly 6 a.m., time to get up. Hebrew lessons would begin in an hour. I lay on my narrow, cot-style bed, waiting for the alarm clock to ring. Across the slender room, Lucie curled up on her bed, face away from me toward the wall, her ribcage swelling and subsiding with each breath. Out of the window, above the orange plastic table, empty except for Lucie's Marlboros, I could see the sky transforming from midnight black to early-morning gray, as dawn began to break.

21
Smoker

The workweek ran from Sunday morning through midday Friday, and by Friday I was spent, as if I'd been doing double workouts with the track team all week. I finished work at the factory, rushed back to my room, stuffed weekend garb into my backpack, and dashed down to the bus stop at the base of the kibbutz. A bus pulled up to the curb. I looked at my backpack and cringed. My gas mask. I had left it in the room.

I walked back to my cabin, picked up my gas mask, and went to the bus stop. The next bus would not come for an hour. I waited on the roadside, watching violet alfalfa buds swing side to side.

The bus came. I boarded, threw my pack above the seat, and clenched the gas mask to my chest. I was going home, to Kiryat Bialik, exhaling as if I'd been holding my breath all week long.

I buzzed the Ben-Artzis's apartment. No one answered. I went in, threw my pack down in Aviv's room, headed to the bathroom, stripped down, took a hot shower, and napped in Moshe's study, waiting for Aviv to come back from school.

I woke to a knock on the door.

"Karol," Moshe said. He opened the door a crack.

"Come in," I said. Groggy.

Moshe shuffled in holding a tray of mint tea, butter cookies, and a tangerine.

"*Ha'kibbutz?*" He asked, wondering about the kibbutz.

"*Zeh tov.*" I said it was good. I lied.

The loneliness that accumulated during the week stayed submerged, but as soon as it was over, the feelings thrust to the surface like a breaching whale. I stayed in Moshe's library, jotting notes about that day and reviewing past entries back to Valentine's Day. It seemed so long ago, but it had only been a week.

February 15. Ofra visits.

February 16. Saw *Pretty Woman* at Kiryon. Target Haifa, Negev nuclear reactor.

February 17. First day on kibbutz. Mostly Russians, except Lucie and me.

February 18. Work in plastics factory. Boss, Ya'akov.

February 19. Meet Lev from Ukraine in Hebrew class. Air raid on kibbutz.

February 20. Read "Shalom, Yitzhak" for homework.

February 21. Eat big lunch. Adaptation to kibbutz.

February 22. Work half-day. Take bus to Kiryat Bialik. Forget gas mask, go back for it.

I dressed and slipped back out to the kiosk.

"Camels," I said.

The clerk handed me a pack, and I walked out toward the agricultural fields a few blocks behind Aviv's home. I moved along a dirt path, through a field of pansies, a purple blanket on either side of my path. I walked and walked and walked until I could hardly see the paved road back to Aviv's. A road full of Renaults and stucco apartments just like his.

Hidden, among all those blooming purple pansies, I crouched on a stone embedded in the dirt path. I picked at the Camels and pulled out a cigarette. Sunshine beat on my forehead, and I ran a finger over my brow. Lined from worry. I lit a cigarette, hand shaking from fatigue, looked out at the pansies, and smoked. Ten cigarettes, one after another, after another. I had not felt so alone since high school when my friend Sarah died.

22
Nine-Point-Two Miles

I did my first long run after Sarah died, so unexpectedly and young. I hadn't planned on it, but I kept running that day and running. I didn't know what else to do. Sarah was my best, best friend back in high school. She was supposed to go to Penn with me, and I didn't know how I'd make it without her. So I ran and ran and ran and clocked more mileage than I'd ever done on a single run. Now I have run marathons and finished Ironman triathlons. Some people think it's insane to swim 2.4 miles, bike 112, and run 26.2, back to back. It's not at all. Endurance sports, for me, are a way of working out life's upsets—big and small. And it all began that summer, after I lost Sarah.

It didn't start out like that. It started out as pure fun in the seventh grade. Before daylight, my father and I used to run through our neighborhood, past all the modest colonial-style homes lined up in a neat row. We lived in Stamford, Connecticut, an hour's commute from my father's office in New York City. I adored morning runs with him, as much as I adored the running itself. The steady beat of my pounding feet, the reliable rhythm of my breathing. In and out. In and out. In and out. It came effortlessly, like a breeze lifted me along, doing all the work, and I had all the fun.

The best runs came after my family moved into a bigger house, a three-story, cedar-sided home with woods on either side and a pond out back. My father and I claimed a five-mile route that wound and dipped and climbed through roads shrouded by maples and oaks and hugged by knee-high fieldstone walls. I never thought that running would hurt, hurt enough to make me cry. But it did. I cried on those hills. Our old neighborhood had long, low-grade hills. They never made me cry. Not once.

Our new neighborhood had brutal, steep, relentless hills. We'd run up three, one after another, along a mile stretch, and in the middle I'd sit down on the curb and weep. "It's so hard," I'd say. My father would stand and wait. "I know, I know," he'd say. He didn't push. He had faith. I'd get up, wipe off my tears, and go. We'd get through the three hills, and then we'd scale the one around the bend that felt nearly vertical. But you knew you had it made when you got to the top. The rest rolled along at easy grades all the way home.

I came to cherish those hills, the hard hills, even when they hurt so badly I thought I'd die. I chugged and huffed and sweat and wept, if need be, until I reached the top. I'd tell myself, over and over, like a coach: *You can do it. You're almost there. You've got what it takes. Don't let yourself down. Keep it going. Pull yourself together. You're a champ. You're a hustler. You're a winner. You're no quitter. Don't do it. Don't quit on a hill.*

In high school, I joined the track team with Kathy. A bleach-blonde, deep-tanned boy magnet who used to eat an orange and go for a five-mile run to stay trim. Kathy quit the team after a week, and I wanted to quit, too. "Oh no," my mother said. She sat across the kitchen table from me and crossed her arms over her chest. She squinted her pale blue eyes and shook her dusty blonde hair. Her cheeks turned pink. "You're not quitting the team. You get back to practice tomorrow, you hear me, Karol Lynn." My mother didn't explain why I had to get back on the team, but I think she worried I'd spend too much time with a curvy girl who attracted too many boys. So I became a hurdler.

Sarah came along in high school after Kathy got sent to Catholic High. I think her mother worried as much as mine about her ability to attract boys, and maybe the nuns would slow things down. Sarah wasn't anything like Kathy. She was skinny, preppy, and shy. Instead of Kathy's blonde bob, Sarah had a cap of chlorine-doused curls—bronze like her eyes. Instead of Kathy's tight jeans and tube tops, Sarah wore chinos and oxfords. Instead of Kathy's bravado with boys, Sarah barely looked them in the eye. I knew Sarah from swim team and orchestra, but I didn't hang out with her. I spent most of my free time with Kathy, sunbathing and waterskiing on the Long Island Sound.

One afternoon, at the beginning of tenth grade, Sarah sat down next to me in study hall, opened her textbook, and started doing her homework. I watched her, amazed. Nobody studied in study hall. What's her deal? I didn't have a problem with studying. I studied, and studied hard. But not here. I studied at home, late at night, in private. Nobody to brand me a geek.

"You study in study hall?" I said.

"Why not?" Sarah said. "That way I don't have to do it later."

"Good point, really good," I said.

She didn't care what people thought of her. And I thought that was cool.

It became a game of who could finish the most school-work before the end of the day. By the time we were seniors, we ranked third and fourth in our class. I always felt a little guilty about being ahead of her in class rank. She worked harder than I did, the way she went about everything. We played in the community youth orchestra together, and I think she practiced her viola a lot more than I did my violin. Still, I played well enough to move to first violin before long. I certainly didn't work as hard as Sarah when it came to swimming, though my half-hearted efforts somehow landed me in the state diving champion-ships every year.

Sarah swam year-round, sometimes twice a day. She'd practice mornings before school at the YMCA, and she'd work out with the Stamford High team in the afternoons. She often swam four or five hours a day, and she almost always won her race. She won the Connecticut state open championships in 100-meter breaststroke our junior and senior years and was named a high school All-American swimmer. And the swim coach at the University of Penn-sylvania recruited her, informally though, since the Ivy League officially prohibits athletic scholarships as if it compromises the higher goals of education. She was planning to go to Penn, like me, and train for the Olympic trials.

Sarah wasn't all books and swimming. Weekends, we would play like rambunctious elementary school children. First, we'd go to the YMCA for a game of racquetball. Afterwards, we'd go for a swim. And then we'd go for a bike ride down by the Long Island Sound. We'd park our bikes and lie down in the sand and talk. Sometimes we talked about boys, like the time we dared each other to ask a boy out. I asked out Matt from life-saving class who became a boyfriend pretty soon. She was supposed to ask out a swimmer from the Y but never did. We didn't spend that much time on boys, though. We spent much more talking about life and how to get through it all right.

"My father is such an asshole," she'd say all the time. He left her and her mother and two brothers when she was a little girl. I couldn't imagine what it would be like to grow up without a father, to me, a friend who provided for me in every way. Sarah's father lived nearby but never visited her or gave her mother money to help out. She'd frown and squint and say it again, "My father is such an asshole." She never told me why she worked as hard as she did, and I never asked. But somehow it seemed understood. She worked hard—Ivy League scholar and Olympic athlete hard—so that someday her father would love her the way mine already did.

I never knew what to say to her at those times, but I knew that being her friend was better than anything I could have said. She wrote in my yearbook next to our swim team photo: "I like myself when I'm with you." She crouched next to me in a huddle pose near the diving board. My study partner, teammate, best friend, until she was so suddenly gone.

I looked for Sarah in AP English. She wasn't there. It was odd that she didn't show. She never missed school. Ever. Not even when she was sick. I wondered what went wrong.

Mr. Kubinec leaned into his desk and crossed his arms over his chest. He dissected *Hedda Gabler*. "Does anyone know what the gun symbolizes?" he asked. The students gawked ahead at him, unsure. "It's a phallic symbol," he said. He flicked his light brown bangs out of his face and turned toward the blackboard. His Levi's hugged his slim hips as he leaned into one socket. He spelled it out on the board: THE GUN = PHALLIC SYMBOL.

The loudspeaker interrupted his lesson. "We have a special announcement," a woman's voice said. "Sarah Jalet's been in a very bad car accident. Let's all please take a moment of silence for her." I sat at my desk near the front of the classroom, staring at Mr. Kubinec's hips. My breath shortened and my heart pounded the way it did after a sprint.

A student knocked on Mr. Kubinec's door. He handed a hall pass to Mr. Kubinec, who waved it at me. "Your guidance counselor wants to see you." He handed me the pass. My guidance counselor knew that Sarah and I were top-ranked students, swim team cocaptains, and best friends. He had recommended both of us to Penn—the Ivy League that he liked to promote—and we were his prize pupils, who were bound to get in. He wanted to make sure that I was okay after hearing about Sarah's bad accident. I felt numb, sitting in that chair. I didn't cry. I didn't even know what to say. What could I tell him? It felt unreal that a person as strong as Sarah could get hurt.

Sarah's mother let me go to the hospital but not into her room. Mrs. Jalet didn't want me to see Sarah with her jaw wired shut. Her mother didn't want me to watch my best friend point to letters on an alphabet pad instead of talking to me. She didn't want me to remember Sarah's broken limbs covered in white plaster or her desperate struggle to breathe with her crushed lungs. I waited outside her room in a reception area, with my mother, on a vinyl green couch.

I thought about the accident, how it happened early morning before school. Sarah drove that winding road to swim practice. A typical Connecticut road that snaked up and around hills, slender curvy paths that used to be for cows. Sarah drove her mother's Volkswagen Beetle, and her little brother, Ben, sat next to her in the passenger seat. Sarah and Ben didn't bother with seatbelts. Connecticut didn't have a law requiring people to strap in, so hardly anybody did back then. A big sedan swerved around a blind corner into Sarah's little bug. The driver had slipped into the oncoming traffic lane while he leaned forward to adjust the heater. Ben hit the passenger side door and broke his leg. Sarah's bony chest smashed into the steering column. Her lungs were crushed.

Sarah's mother looked at me with her big, brown eyes. Her black hair had streaks of silver, but her tawny skin had no lines at all, still fleshy and smooth like a young woman's. "You don't want to go in there, honey," she said. "You really don't."

I held up the card I brought for Sarah. "Can you bring this to her?"

"Sure I can."

"When do you think she'll be out?"

Mrs. Jalet looked at me, her eyelids hung low and sad, and they told me more than I wanted to know.

"We're not sure, honey—we're just not sure."

Mrs. Jalet didn't call. I found out from Gary, my running partner. He walked toward me on the indoor pool deck. I worked as a lifeguard at the Italian Center, keeping guard on a folding chair near the pool office. It was early spring, and outdoor swimming was still months away.

"Have you heard?" he said.

"About what?" I said. My knees pulled up to my chest, one eye on Gary's lean face and the other on the lap swimmers, most of them seniors taking easy strokes up and down the pool.

"Sarah," he said. He looked at me and paused. "She died."

Gary sat with me in quiet support, the way he ran with me, patient like my father, up the big hills that used to make me cry. I watched the woman who swam two miles a day. She was over sixty, but you wouldn't take her for more than forty or forty-five at most. She had these ever-blushing cheeks that made her perpetual smile seem even warmer. She smiled before she got into the pool, and she smiled when she got out. She even smiled when she told me one day, after I'd asked why she swam so much, that she swam because her husband and son had died.

That summer, after losing Sarah, I went out for a run. I planned to do the usual five-mile loop, but when I cleared that last patch of hills and headed toward the easy downhill homestretch, I didn't feel worn-out, too far from tired to forget the ache of missing Sarah. I did an about-face and headed back toward another pack of hills, steeper ones I'd never run before. I loped along, moving under the shade of dense green leaves. Oaks and maples formed an archway of branches above me, a protection from the yellow summer sun beating through the greenery in scattered beams. The road inclined up and up, hardly a break in its slope. I wound around a curve, looped back down, and then ran my usual route in reverse. Later, I drove the distance in my father's Peugeot and checked the odometer. Nine-point-two miles.

23
Litmus Test

Scuds had exploded around Haifa, Tel Aviv, the West Bank, the Negev Desert, and the Mediterranean Sea—hitting homes, apartment buildings, a basement bomb shelter, leather factory, jewelry store, school for handicapped children, Ha'Maccabiah Stadium, Yarkon National Park, and the Lev Ha'Mifratz Shopping Mall still under construction in Haifa Bay. The Gulf War ended on Purim, a celebration of the biblical story of Esther, the queen who foils a plot to kill the Jews. It was a fitting time for the war to end. I found out from Jeremy in the morning before Hebrew class on the kibbutz. He told me that ground troops had liberated Kuwait in one hundred hours. He'd read about it in the newspaper. There would be no more air raids. It was all over.

It came as a letdown. I wanted the end of the war to be big, like an Independence Day celebration, full of fireworks, champagne, kisses, hugs, shouts for joy. Instead, it came by word of mouth. Like, Oh, didn't you hear? Some bit of gossip. Nothing too important. It seemed so out of proportion to the six long weeks of air raids that had sent us running to the sealed room, breathing under gas masks that brewed nausea in our guts, listening to Scuds explode in Haifa and the surrounding bay, staring at atropine needles and decontamination powder, wondering if we would need to use them. Swallowing the awful loneliness of war.

I felt cheated.

After it was all over, no one spoke about it. It was as if it hadn't happened. Even memory of that time fell into a black hole. But the soul didn't forget. A couple years after the war, while driving through suburban New York, a fire alarm went off. I burst into tears. It wasn't a fire alarm, to me. It was an air-raid siren. I had to run to the sealed room. When hijackers brought down the twin towers on September 11, 2001, I was on one of the first trains out of Manhattan. Later, my brother-in-law teased, "Karol was like, 'The Scuds are coming, the Scuds are coming.'" I had to be out of there.

I spent the weekend with Aviv, and when I returned to the kibbutz, I found Lucie in bed with the covers pulled over her head.

I nudged her. "Is everything all right?"

She pulled the covers down. "I am sick from too much drinking."

I sat on the edge of my bed across from her.

Lucie sat up and stared at me, blank.

"Did something happen?"

She drew her knees to her chest, hugged her arms around her calves, and burrowed her face in her thighs.

She began to sob, rocking back and forth, as if saying yes with her whole body.

"Jeremy, he rapes me," she said.

I leapt up and hugged her. It took her a long time to stop rocking and crying. When she did, I sat down next to her and put my arm around her. Then she told me what happened.

"I am playing poker and drinking with Jeremy, like always when you are gone from the kibbutz. He is my friend, you know, when you are staying with Aviv. So after we are finishing our poker game, Jeremy comes to my room. We are talking, you know, and then suddenly he tells me he wants to make love. I tell him, 'No, I have a boyfriend in France.' He doesn't say anything. He turns me around, pulls down my pants, and goes in from behind." She grimaced and gestured with her hands as she described what Jeremy had done. "The neighbors hear me crying. They start knocking on the door, asking if I am okay. I don't answer. I make him leave through the window."

"Have you told anyone?" I asked.

"I only tell you."

"We have to tell someone. The ulpan directors or the kibbutz psychologist."

"I don't want to tell. People will say I shouldn't be alone with him in my room."

"He's your friend. Why shouldn't he be here?" I said.

Lucie sobbed. And I sat with her, wondering what I should do. "We have to do something," I said.

Lucie wiped her eyes, sniffed, and looked at me, like a child wanting her mother to make it better.

"Cow dung in his boots," I said.

Lucie's lip quivered. Then she let out a hoot. I did, too, and soon we were bent into our knees, belly laughing.

At midnight, we slid on our work boots, snuck down to the factory, and crept through an open window. We fumbled in the dark for plastic bags and scrap refrigerator shelf lips, leftovers from my work in the factory, where I sliced long silvery strips of scrap plastic into sections of trim. We crawled back out of the window and slipped down to the cow pen. It smelled like dung. I stuck the refrigerator shelf lip into a pile of excrement and scooped it into a plastic bag, one heaping clump after another until I had enough to fill his boots. "Done," I whispered. Then we snuck up to Jeremy's cottage. As usual, he had left his knee-high rubber boots on the doorstep.

"They're there," I said, pointing to the boots. "Let's make sure they're asleep." We slipped around the rear of the cottage to peer through the window. The lights were out. "He's snoring, listen," I said. Lucie put her hand over her mouth, giggled. "Come on," I said. We tiptoed back to the porch. I set the bag down, stuck in the plastic strip and scooped dung into his boots, one clump at a time. "Let's go," I said. We ran back to our cabin, shut the door.

I had dung on my hands and boots, a criminal, breaking, entering, robbing, vandalizing. Now I needed to hide the evidence.

Lucie was my accomplice. She had followed me around, a silent partner, to the factory, the cow pen, Jeremy's cottage, and now the showers. We washed our bodies and boots, laughed some more, and, for the moment, the pain seemed forgotten. Forgotten in fun. Mischievous fun without consequences. Jeremy thought one of the Russians had filled his boots with dung in a drunken frenzy. A meaningless prank. We didn't tell our secret, or his.

I called Aviv, sobbing, whispering into the dining room pay phone spare details about what had happened. I didn't want anyone to overhear. Under normal circumstances, I could have handled this. I had been trained to deal with problems like date rape as a resident advisor at Penn, and during the middle of the night a freshman had knocked on my door to try to tell me that her roommate had been date raped. Not knowing what she wanted to tell me, I asked if it could wait until morning, and by the time I found out what had happened, she had dropped out of school. Back then, I couldn't understand how someone could quit school because her roommate had been date raped, because the truth is my first time happened with someone I'd just met at a fraternity party, and he didn't stop when I said, "No, I've never done this before." He called the next day and wanted to see me, and while he was as sexy cool as James Dean, I told him again that I hadn't done that before and wasn't going to do it again. "I thought you were making it up," he said. But these were not normal times, and now, finally, I had snapped, a rubber band stretched too far.

It would be years before I understood the intensity of my response to Lucie's rape, coming so soon after the end of the war, provoking the same feelings of helplessness and isolation, terror and rage, that Aviv and I'd had during the air raids, feelings that didn't go away when the war ended, feelings that would haunt us long after it was over, the way they sometimes haunt survivors of war and terrorism and natural disasters as well as rape and assault and accidents and their witnesses, like journalists and photographers and anyone touched by trauma. The terrorist attacks in Mumbai and New York City, the wars in Iraq and Afghanistan, the civil wars in Rwanda and the former Yugoslavia, the hurricane in New Orleans, the earthquakes in China and Haiti and those that propelled the tsunamis in Japan and the Indian Ocean. But back then I thought that combat stress, shell shock, battle fatigue was only something that veterans of long and deadly wars could suffer, like veterans of Vietnam and Korea and the World Wars. No, I didn't know then that a winter-long war could hurt, too.

Aviv drove to the kibbutz and stayed overnight in our cabin, sleeping on my slender cot with me. I curled into him, his warmth soothing me, his cheek pressing against mine. Lucie looked at us, moist eyes, smiling. Maybe that one night Lucie and I both felt safe, but her rape had broken me, crippled my drive to fit in. I knew I couldn't go on. I couldn't handle secrets. Any secrets. Big or small. I always told. Told on my sister. Told on my brother. Even told on myself sometimes. I wasn't a rat, exactly, but I thought I'd explode like a balloon too full of air unless I told. Like the time my brother showed me the peanut butter sandwich he'd made to stash his pot in on a high school band trip. I didn't want to tell on my brother, not at all. But the story pressed and pressed and pressed on me, until I thought I really was a balloon ready to burst. And then I blurted it out to my mother.

Lucie's story made me swell up, full of secrets, the way my brother's peanut butter sandwich had, only worse.

With my brother I didn't worry at all that he'd become a pothead. I just couldn't keep it in. Plain as that. But with Lucie, I felt a moral urgency to tell. Maybe I am telling her story now only to unburden myself from having had to stuff it away all this time. She wanted me to tell no one, only I am sure she guessed I told Aviv, with him sleeping across from her that night, in bed with me, comforting me with soft kisses and whispers about how soon we would be back in New York, back where everything would be okay, like it was before.

I'd felt a certain moral mission to fly to Israel on the eve of the Gulf War, an act of heroism I hoped would gain favor with Aviv's parents, Moshe and Sarah. An act to prove that I could cut it, that I could handle war and terror and all that Israel was about. I wanted to prove that I wasn't a traitor, like the Israelis who fled during war or never came home when it was under fire. I wanted to show that I could understand and cherish their world, and all the history that had shaped it. I wanted to learn a whole new alphabet and speak in Hebrew, to talk with Moshe and Sarah and Aviv in their own tongue. I wanted to work hard on the kibbutz, show my colors through my solid and steady fitting and slicing and tossing. My perfect refrigerator shelf lips. I wanted to write about the constant relentless terror, the air raids, and the threat of chemical and biological warfare.

And I did. Did all that. Learned how to write a letter and speak in Hebrew. Cut plastic like a professional machinist on the kibbutz. Weathered a war without fleeing. And sold stories to my Connecticut newspaper on the intifada and the Gulf War. All of that had a moral purpose. But Lucie's rape was different. I couldn't muster any noble reason for keeping her secret, not at all. It felt like a dirty skeleton, the kind inmates must hold onto after prison rapes. A skeleton I carried in my backpack, trudging around hoping someone would find it and ask what it was. A secret that had no place to be told.

I ducked as Aviv ferried me out of the kibbutz. He drove past the alfalfa fields, still lolling back and forth. A lullaby.

"I can deal with a lot of things, a whole lot," I sniffed. "But this? This is different. I can't. Can't handle it. Not one bit."

I shook my head, side to side, thinking no, no, no. I won't abide this secret. It's not right, not right at all. I bent into my knees and wept, wrenching and sobbing and gasping.

Aviv steered his father's Renault, gripping the wheel so tight his knuckles turned white. He stared dead-on at the road. "I hate that my country does this to you."

"I'm not going back," I said. "I can't, I can't, I can't."

I hid like an escaped convict after I left the kibbutz. I slept through the night and into the next day, the way I did after the late-night bombings during the war, coming out of Aviv's bedroom only late at night, after Moshe and Sarah had gone to sleep. I couldn't face them. I knew how it would disappoint them if I quit, but I couldn't go back. Ever. So I holed up for four days. Aviv's bedroom was no longer the sealed room. The window no longer had a big plastic tarp to protect us from shattering glass. The radio was no longer on all the time, no longer tuned to the "silent station" that broadcast the air-raid siren when Scuds were on the way. The room no longer had gas masks, flashlights, batteries, bottled water, crackers, damp towels, masking tape—things we had needed to survive a chemical attack. Aviv had put everything away, back where it belonged, because the war was over.

I found Sarah on the enclosed balcony off the dining room. She sat in a rocking chair knitting. Her blonde bob always so neat, like a television news anchor's.

"Shalom," I said.

"Shalom," she said, looking up over her reading glasses.

I didn't want to have the conversation in Hebrew, even though I probably could have. It seemed too important, and I wasn't sure that I knew all the right words to describe what had happened on the kibbutz and how I felt. So I continued in English.

"I'm not going back to the kibbutz," I said.

She set down her knitting. "Why?"

I told her about Lucie.

She furrowed her brow. "But was this really rape?"

Sarah's question hit me like a missile. I could forgive her and Moshe for not comforting me after the air raids. It would be as unlikely as a group of soldiers hugging and consoling each other after a battle. I understood, enough, that it wasn't the Israeli thing to do. But this, to me, was different, very different. Lucie was my roommate, my friend, a young woman. Vulnerable, violated. And Sarah was a mother, my mother away from home. How could she abandon me?

My shoulders pinched together. "She wasn't beaten or bruised, if that's what you mean. But the guy took her against her will. That's rape, as far as I'm concerned."

Sarah no longer seemed soft, the way she had at first, when she spoke to me like a confidante, a girlfriend she could tell anything in the world. Now she stared at me with cold, unfeeling eyes that made my stomach clench. I couldn't bear the disapproval of mothers. Aviv's or my own.

"When I am young, like you, I am also so sensitive, so sensitive I cry over anything, any feeling that I do not like," Sarah said. "I hear you cry, and I worry because you are so sensitive, so sensitive like I was when I was young."

"I know, I know, I'm sensitive, I try not to be," I said.

My mother used to call me Sensitive Plant after the type of mimosa whose tiny fernlike leaves wither into its stem at the slightest touch. Growing up, I wanted her approval so badly that any criticism crushed me. Now I wanted Sarah's approval and compassion. It hurt like mad that I wasn't getting it. Wasn't getting my medal after the war. Instead, I was getting a reprimand like I got from my own mother for being a Sensitive Plant she had to handle with care.

"I worry you are so sensitive, and I worry that maybe my son is not always nice with you," Sarah said. "Is he nice with you?"

"Yes, yes, he's nice to me. He's my best friend," I said. I did not want to tell her how things had strained between Aviv and me, but maybe she already knew. We never went out anymore, never did the kinds of things we'd done in New York. We hardly ever went to a movie, or out for cappuccino and cheesecake, or for a walk through the agricultural fields, that place on the outskirts of town where I'd smoked and cried on a rock among the pansies. We hardly left home for anything apart from Aviv attending classes at school and my afternoon runs, as if waiting in limbo until his semester ended and we could get back to New York.

Sarah cupped her knitting in her lap. She looked at me for a long while without speaking. She gave me the kind of look my mother would give me when she worried that I was heading down a path that would hurt me. "I had to learn to be strong," Sarah said. "Strong like a good Israeli girl has to be strong. We have no time for crying. If we are crying, then we will cry every day. Yes, the war is over, but only for now. Tomorrow will come something new. Always, always something new. So I learn, I learn not to cry. And I am strong now so I can survive, you see?"

I sniffed and nodded my head. "Yes, I want to be strong."

I wanted to endure the war, the kibbutz, Israel. All of it. But it felt like a litmus test, and I was failing—turning basic blue instead of acidic pink.

24

Better to Smile

Aviv signed me up for a city ulpan. It was at the elementary school he'd attended as a child, and the school where his mother had taught. There were a dozen of us, everyone from the Soviet Union, except me. I sat in the back next to Boris from Azerbaijan. He looked like a cherub. Blond, blue-eyed, and boyish. Mornings, I'd ride Aviv's bike to school and park it near the playground. During breaks, I'd walk to the mall and smoke. Afternoons I'd go to a café in the mall and read. Eventually, I'd pack up, smoke another cigarette or two, and ride back to Aviv's. I'd usually make it back about the time that Aviv was returning from school.

On Holocaust Remembrance Day an air-raid siren wailed in the morning, and we had two minutes of silence. Afterwards, Na'amah, the teacher, showed us a video. It was the kind I'd seen as an elementary school student in Connecticut. Nazis, concentration camps, gas chambers, corpses, and emaciated survivors. I went home early that day, and the rest of the week, to watch movies about the Holocaust.

Like *Voyage of the Damned*, a feature about a boat of Jewish Germans fleeing Nazis. The ship was turned away by Cuba, and then by the United States. And *Shoah*—"the catastrophe"—Claude Lanzmann's nine-and-a-half-hour documentary. One of the survivors of Chelmno—a Nazi death camp in Poland—who now lived in Israel, smiled easily and often, and the filmmaker wondered why. "Sometimes you smile, sometimes you cry. And if you're alive, it's better to smile." I wanted to smile, too, but I wept through every film. It was no longer a history lesson, to me. It was Moshe and Sarah and Aviv's history, and it had become personal, thinking of the children Aviv and I would have, of how I had to protect them from a cruel and prejudiced world.

I wept for those who died in the Holocaust, and for the first time I felt the full weight of those who had died in war, like Wilson, my father's good friend in Vietnam, a hilarious hillbilly about to get court-martialed when my father began to mentor him. My father had become the fire direction officer of the battery, teaching Wilson how to read maps and provide coordinates for the gun crews firing artillery, white phosphorous, and antipersonnel rounds from the howitzers. The night before Wilson was killed, the men arrived at a new location so late that Wilson's commander took pity on his men and didn't make them dig in. The North Vietnamese ambushed the battery at dawn, shooting up foxholes along the perimeter and then the fire direction tent where Wilson slept. My father won the Bronze Star for Valor in Battle for running to the gun pit and ordering the antipersonnel round that stopped the attack, after the big guns spewed tiny darts toward the enemy soldiers, who let out agonized screams. When the battle was over, my father found Wilson lying on the floor of the fire direction tent, staring toward my father with glassy eyes. "I'll be back soon," my father said, but later he realized that Wilson was probably already dead. "It was such a waste," my father would say, and he'd tear up every time. My father tried to teach me about the sense-lessness of war by telling stories about his tour in Vietnam, but I had to learn, too. My understanding began as raw emotion, welling up whenever I was reminded of war and death and loss, and feeling shame about the depth of my sorrow because what I'd gone through during the Gulf War seemed so insignificant compared to other, much more violent wars; but eventually I would see how devastating even a short and "surgical" war can be.

Over the next fifteen years, eleven thousand Gulf War veterans from the United States would die and more than two hundred thousand—about a third of the surviving vet-erans—would go on disability, suffering from a range of conditions such as chronic fatigue, muscle and joint pain, skin rashes, and memory loss; and children of veterans, born after the war, would suffer birth defects. While sci-entific studies would find that the only common thread was psychological stress, veterans may have suffered from toxic exposure from chemical bunker demolitions, deplet-ed uranium antitank artillery used by coalition troops, pyridostigmine bromide anti–nerve gas pills, anthrax and botulinum toxin vaccinations, pesticides, insecticides, and oil well fires set by Iraqi soldiers at the end of the war.

But none of the Scuds fired at Saudi Arabia or Israel contained lethal liquids, gases, or germs. In all thirty-nine Scuds struck Israel over thirty-nine days, sending us to shelters and sealed rooms eighteen times, including eight times during the Jewish Sabbath. The attacks damaged forty-one hundred buildings and as many as twelve thousand apartments—destroying at least twenty-eight buildings and as many as four hundred apartments—including some damage from Patriot explosions and falling debris. But only 2 people died from a missile explosion. Another 5 died from heart attacks brought on by the attacks and 7 from suffocation under their gas masks. Eleven were seriously wounded; 220 were lightly injured, and 815 were treated for acute anxiety, unnecessary atropine injections, and injuries from rushing to shelters and sealed rooms.

The casualties were much lower than expected, considering the fear that hundreds or thousands would die in a chemical and biological attack, and the fact that at least 1,150 Iranians had died and 4,000 were injured from 135 conventional Scud attacks on Tehran toward the end of the Iran-Iraq War. At the time, I thought that the Patriot had shielded us, but a Massachusetts Institute of Technology study would later find that it probably had more to do with reinforced concrete, early warnings, evacuations, nighttime attacks, and "good fortune." People were buried under rubble but only suffered light injuries. An air-raid shelter took a direct hit but nobody was inside. And several of the warheads were duds.

The worst Scud attack was in Saudi Arabia, where a Scud punched through the roof of a military barracks in Dahran, killing twenty-eight—an improbable bull's-eye that was the single deadliest attack against coalition forces, which lost about four hundred men and women during the Gulf War. Those who died in the thousands were Iraqi—including about twenty thousand soldiers and two thousand civilians, who became known as "collateral damage," like those who perished when coalition bombs accidentally struck homes, apartment buildings, commercial complexes, hotels, hospitals, schools, markets, a mosque, and the Ameriyya air-raid shelter.

Na'amah let us break for lunch, and I walked out with Natalia. She looked like a babushka, a round-faced peasant. She took a liking to me and began asking about Aviv, his studies, our plans to marry. She tried to include me with the other women who gathered during breaks, but often I excused myself for a smoke and a short walk to the Kiryon Mall. I'd always had a fiercely independent streak, eating alone in my college cafeteria so that I didn't have to coordinate my schedule with anyone else. But now I was retreating into myself, the way Moshe and Sarah had during the war, because it felt as if layers of my skin had been peeled back and almost anything hurt. Being alone relaxed me, but I had grown fond of Natalia, and this day I sat with her on a bench and watched Boris and the other men play basketball. It was the same court that Aviv had played on as an elementary school boy.

Natalia crossed her arms over her chest and told me about her friend, a Ukrainian woman who lived with her husband on a moshav, a cooperative farm similar to a kibbutz but more commercial. She was studying with an Orthodox rabbi to convert but kept quiet about the fact that she wasn't Jewish. "My friend, she is crying every day," Natalia said. She looked at me and continued. "In Russia, nobody cares about mixed marriage. In Israel, this is problem. If mother isn't Jewish, baby isn't Jewish. Problem. Big problem."

I nodded, sympathetic, but felt isolated, confused, and strangely mute, unable to articulate the source of sorrow because by then the war and even Lucie's rape had slipped from consciousness, an automatic form of self-preservation that erases memories too troubling to hold but carelessly misses the heart. I wanted to tell her how Aviv and I had worked out the terms of our marriage long ago, how we never argued about our differences in religion and culture, how we saw each other's humanity above all. She was so kind, so motherly, but I had no stamina left to tell her any of that or how so often people only thought of the problems of a mixed marriage when they thought of us, as if our struggles could be reduced to the choice of conversion and the adoption of customs, as if we hadn't wrestled with the larger questions of war and terrorism and violence, the more elusive existential demands of everyday life in Israel. After class, I biked to the pansy fields, smoked, and decided to quit the ulpan. This time I told Moshe.

Moshe leaned over his desk, burrowed in documents, diligently working on his memoir. I handed him a letter in simple Hebrew telling him that I had quit the ulpan, explaining how Natalia's discussion about conversion had been too much for me, because the truth is Aviv had told me not to tell anyone in the city ulpan that I wasn't Jewish, a lie of omission that had made it easier for me to transfer from the kibbutz ulpan but a lie that made it impossible for me to truly befriend Natalia or anyone else at school, a lie that I could no longer bear. I sat down on the couch, now pushed along the wall, below his books. He read the letter, bent into it, the way he had his documents. Then he looked up, knitting his brow. He ran his hand over his bare forehead as if smoothing his hair, though he had none there to smooth. I knew I had disappointed him by quitting the kibbutz and my Hebrew lessons, and I expected him to be hard on me like Sarah had been. But he wasn't. He was gentle, compassionate, concerned.

"I worry," Moshe said in Hebrew, and then he paused. "I worry that Aviv does not understand the pressures of a mixed marriage."

"I know," I said, feeling instant regret at having betrayed Aviv but also enormous relief at finally being able to have a frank discussion with Moshe in his own language, so I continued the conversation in Hebrew. "Aviv always says it will be fine once we get back to New York, but I worry that maybe we will have problems there, too. Maybe we won't be happy like we were before."

"Aviv thinks it's so easy in America, but I think it's not so easy as he thinks. I think he's too young to marry." Moshe looked at me like an anxious father, protective, probing. I knew that Moshe wasn't concerned about conversion, being an atheist like Aviv. He worried instead that Aviv would lose his identity by leaving Israel, diluting his connection to his culture and language and land, and he would carry this discussion on with his son even after we returned to New York. One of his letters would send Aviv deep into despair. "I tell my father that I love you as a human being, and in this letter my father says, 'If your wife is a human being.' My father uses the Hebrew word for *if.*" Aviv was so sensitive, like me, and I knew that his father was simply posing a philosophical question about the nature of identity and the taboo of *yoridah*—"going down," leaving Israel. It was a question worth asking, a question that didn't hurt me at all because I knew that his only concern was for his son's well-being, and because I knew well the pressures of adapting to another culture, the challenge to the core self, the struggle to find a comfortable path that cherishes the old and embraces the new, and that the time Aviv had spent in New York, nearly a year all told, was like the year I'd spent in Argentina, where I was just passing through, never trying to become Argentine, rebelling against a culture that wanted women to strive for supermodel beauty. But the six months in Israel, seven before I would go home, felt like years instead of months, because I had tried so hard to adapt to Aviv's culture, to learn Hebrew for Moshe, to be strong for Sarah, to become an Israeli, a *sabra*, a good soldier, and I felt like a dropout, a quitter, a failure.

Like I felt when we we'd celebrated Passover at Ofra's in-laws. She looked like a compact version of Aviv, golden-brown hair and a long narrow face. Her name means "fawn" in Hebrew. It fit. She was upbeat, friendly, the good girl who never gave Sarah and Moshe any trouble. Everyone greeted us with kisses and hugs, and soon we were at the dining room table for the seder. The prayer book went around the table. Everyone read a section and passed it on. It came to me. Moshe smiled, eager to show off his pupil. I stared at the Hebrew text, like a dyslexic. Hebrew not only reads right to left, but most vowel sounds are implied, so the beginner can't lumber through texts with phonetic pronunciations. Aviv took the book and passed it along. That was months ago, but as good as my Hebrew had become, good enough to have my first talk with Moshe about his son, marriage, life in America, I knew I was still a disappointment.

25
Hermit Crab

The house was silent, apart from Aviv turning textbook pages and Moshe tapping the computer keyboard. At first, I'd admired the cerebral tone in Moshe's home. Now I wanted out of that house, the way I had wanted out of the library back in college. The silence choked me, crippled my thoughts, and sent me running to the student union. I needed coffee and bagels, laughter and chatter, the constant flow of people coming, going, sipping, sighing, burping, scratching, and fussing around. I thrived on the chaos of things.

"This isn't a home, it's a library," I said.

I tossed the newspaper down on the bed and stared out of the window at Aviv's garden below. "I have to get out of this house," I said. "I'm suffocating."

Aviv focused on his textbook, shoulders slumped.

"Are you going to work all weekend long?" I said. "I can't stand it. We never go out anymore."

I grabbed my backpack and ran downstairs to the garden. I pulled out my Camels and lit a cigarette. Aviv rushed downstairs and found me in the garden, comforting me like always about how it would be better in New York, how we would be happy again. We'd had fights back in New York, too, but we'd always worked things out quickly and constructively, and it was so comforting to me, coming from a family with parents who were always in some sort of standoff. Back then, my father would become morose about work, having idealized the business world as a place that was blissfully free of the political jockeying that had soured him on the army, and my mother would eventually rip into him for his quiet ways of taking the stress out on her. It would take years for my father to learn how to let his worries go, but once he did, he found that things worked out far better than he imagined both at work and with my mother.

Growing up, I felt weary from their fights, and when I was a teenager, my father would turn to me, slumping in the driver's seat before we'd go out for a Dr. Pepper, and ask, "Am I such a bad guy?" "No, Dad, you're a great guy!" I'd say, too young to absorb the complexities of their relationship, something I would not understand until I found myself losing patience with Aviv, whose anger during the air raids had morphed into melancholy now that they were over. And our fights were no longer quick and constructive, like the ones we had in New York.

We broke up for a few days because Aviv hadn't shown any interest in my articles. "I don't like politics," he said. "But you read the Israeli papers, and besides, they aren't all about politics." We didn't speak for several days, and when he finally called, he said that he wanted to read all my stories. He handed me a rose, and I handed him a big stack of articles published in the Connecticut newspaper, the Buenos Aires weekly, the Argentine American Chamber of Commerce magazine and newsletter, the Penn foreign affairs journal. He read them all and then helped me think up story ideas. "Why don't you write about Taquile?" he said. So I wrote a story about how islanders threw rocks to protest mainland boats taking tourists to the island; how they wanted to ferry their own tourists to pay for coffee, sugar, supplies; how Aviv and his friends made a protest sign for them; and how they celebrated by playing soccer. The story would run beside my op-ed about the election of President Alberto Fujimori, a college professor who had defeated the novelist and future Nobel Laureate, Mario Vargas Llosa.

We also had run-ins about "okay." "Did you like the movie?" "It was okay," he'd say. "Do you like my outfit?" "It's okay." "Do you think I'm beautiful?" "You're okay." "Okay, just okay?" I got huffy. "What do you mean just okay?" "Elle Macpherson is beautiful. You're okay, like me." We had a heated exchange about it, even though I figured he was evening the score after I'd told him about Andy. But it was more than that. Americans tend to say exuberant things, like excellent, fantastic, wonderful, while Israelis tend to say *beseder*, "okay," for just about everything. He wasn't going to use the word *beautiful* unless a supermodel was involved. It wasn't the Israeli thing to do. So I let it go. It didn't bother me much. I already knew what he thought about my looks. He took photos of me all the time, pinned them above his desk, even made a T-shirt out of one of my childhood shots. Later, I called up my college roommate Lenore told her the story, and she said, "But you look like Elle Macpherson." Lenore's the only friend who thought so. Most often, people have told me that I look like Juliette Lewis, an actress who's too short and scrappy to be a supermodel. Once, a man sat down next to me at the counter of the diner below my apartment in Manhattan and said, "I know who you are. You're that actress."

"No, I'm not Juliette Lewis."

"Okay, right, I understand," he said, nodding his head as if respecting her privacy.

When it came to the big things, like where to live and how to raise children, we didn't so much fight as negotiate. While I'd cherished my years in the Christian Science Sunday school, I easily agreed when Aviv asked me not to take our children to church, knowing how strongly he felt about organized religion, even his own. Aviv had bristled when he found out that Caroline, one of my best friends from college who was the daughter of an American artist and an Israeli contractor who'd settled in Miami, had married an Orthodox Jewish boy while we were still in school and had become so religious herself that she kept kosher and strictly observed the Sabbath. I'd go over to Caroline and Jay's apartment in the married student housing on Saturdays, talking and laughing and sharing hallah for hours, after watching Jay put on his prayer shawl and daven.

"And this guy is praying, 'Thank God he doesn't make me a woman,'" Aviv said. I wanted to defend my friends, knowing they were among the most compassionate and spiritually minded people I knew, but I deferred to Aviv, because he was careful with facts, so careful that he became a world civilization teaching assistant at City College while finishing his undergraduate coursework. Eventually, I would ask Caroline about it, and she would say, "That's a prayer, and there's also a prayer that thanks God for not making me a goy or a slave." We laughed, as usual, and then she explained her interpretation. "Women bear children so they are already close to God, but men need to pray constantly to feel close to Him."

It had never troubled me because I knew that it was the spirit behind someone's faith that mattered, and I also knew that Aviv's disdain for religion was a natural response to the fanaticism in the Middle East. So I didn't argue with him about religion, since by then I, too, had fallen away from church. I'd been a faithful Sunday school student all through college, looking forward to classes with Sidney Luce, an insightful man who'd worked as a businessman in the Middle East and had become a personal friend of Ginger Rogers. Despite inspiring teachers like Mr. Luce, I'd always been sensitive to the undercurrent of hypocrisy that can be found in any organized religion. I'd attended all five Christian Science churches in Buenos Aires without ever committing to one and finally stopped going altogether after an usher in Manhattan glared at me for wearing faded blue jeans to church.

We had always worked things out with such ease, mostly because neither of us argued with the other when we felt strongly about something. Aviv wanted to spend our engagement in Israel, and I agreed wholeheartedly. I wanted to finish graduate school in New York, and Aviv agreed to transfer to a school there, applying to Hunter College like his sister had, though he would end up at City College, where admissions were open, because the wartime closing of his university had caused his transcripts to arrive too late for Hunter. Aviv didn't want a church wedding because he said it would hurt his parents, and I agreed to get married at City Hall in Manhattan.

Now we quarreled over small slights, like the one about Aviv's old girlfriend who invited us to her wedding. Amit lived down the street and had dated Aviv in high school. I was curious about her. Wondered if she was beautiful, but of course, Aviv would only say that she was "okay." Moshe, Sarah, Aviv, and I sat at a table in the wedding hall. In the center was the huppah. Amit came out in a white wedding dress and gracefully walked to the huppah. She was pretty, petite, brunette. The girl next door. "She is such a lovely girl," Sarah said. "Ima," Aviv said. Sarah looked at Aviv and sighed. That night, I took it out on Aviv, even though it was a small slight, the sort that my mother had endured from my father's mother for her entire marriage, my grandmother always preferring my father's old girlfriend Mary Jo to my mother.

Aviv was calm and comforting about Amit, but weeks later he blew up over our wedding invitations. His sister Ofra designed swimsuits for a living, and we figured she'd do something hip for us. Instead, she illustrated a little boy and girl, cheeks puffy with baby fat. "You've got to be kidding," I said. "This looks like an invitation to a toddler's birthday party." Aviv sat on the bed, shoulders drooped. "This isn't what I expected," he said. Aviv shot up off the bed, rushed into the living room, and ripped into his father and mother about the invitations. It exploded into a huge fight about how he was no longer a baby. Moshe wanted to parcel out the money he'd saved for

Aviv's education, semester by semester, but Aviv wanted it all up front before he moved to New York. It was only ten thousand shekels, worth almost ten thousand U.S. dollars depending on the fluctuating exchange rate, but it seemed like an enormous amount of money at the time. Aviv had always been so rational and even-keel, but that afternoon he yelled and yelled and yelled, while I hid in his bedroom behind the marbled-glass door.

Aviv didn't ever lash out at me, but he withdrew silently to his books. He'd come home from school, sit in front of the computer, and work all night. Night after night after night. Friday would come, and I'd be starved for affection, and again he'd turn on the computer. It wasn't like him. Back in New York, he'd always been the one to pull me out of the house—to catch a movie, chat at a café, see live jazz, dance at a club, explore the city. Like the day we went to Fort Greene to see Spike Lee's store. Aviv was the guy who made happy faces out of fruit, who nurtured me as tenderly as he did his garden. But now, weekends would come, and he only wanted to study. "I can't take it anymore, we never go out," I would say. He'd pick a movie, halfheartedly, and we'd go out, but it wasn't the same without his enthusiasm and curiosity and creativity, the kind he expressed in his drawings, like the flamenco dancer he'd penciled on his bedroom wall as a teenager, our backs covering the sketch when we huddled together in the sealed room.

"Are we going to be happy again?" I would ask again and again, and he'd assure me every time that we would be happy once we got back to New York. I wanted to believe him, but I felt uneasy, raw, and then one night I blew. We'd gone to see the film *Not without My Daughter*, about an American woman whose Iranian husband becomes fanatical after the revolution breaks out in Iran, and she's trapped in the country with her daughter, struggling to get both of them out. "They shoot this film in Israel," Aviv said, his cocky tone chafing against my exposed nerves, having identified with the woman caught in a war and a culture that disapproved of her. I was so worked up that I told Aviv that I felt like that with his family, remembering how Revital hadn't wanted Aviv to marry me, how Moshe had been so stern during our Hebrew lessons, how Sarah had been so hard when I'd quit the kibbutz. Aviv was incensed, and we argued the whole way home, so that by the time we arrived in the garden of Moshe and Sarah's apartment building, I had lost all objectivity and rationality and perspective about my circumstances and began to pound on his chest in a violent outburst of rage and despair and sheer exhaustion.

"I can't take this anymore. I'm going home. I'm buying a ticket to New York. I'm leaving tomorrow," I said, bawling into his shoulder as he held me close.

"Don't go, please don't go. I love you," he said.

Aviv said we should go to therapy. Nadav's father was a psychologist, and Aviv asked him for a recommendation. He suggested Tovah, a family therapist in Haifa. She had an office in her home on Mount Carmel near Aviv's university. She had a hip shag haircut, warm brown eyes, and a round motherly face. She put me at ease. "So what is the problem here?" she said. Aviv and I looked at each other.

"We're fighting a lot," I said.

"Why are you fighting?" she said.

Aviv and I shrugged.

"We fought about wedding invitations the other day," I said, too blocked and confused and defensive to bring up our fight after the movies, my sense of failure for quitting the ulpan, my collapse following Lucie's rape, my terrifying loneliness during the air raids, Aviv's anger about being "sitting ducks," and both of our tears. Too timid to tell Nadav's father's colleague such shameful things. Aviv didn't say much to Tovah, either, as a reserve soldier in the Israeli army who could get kicked out of the military for being emotionally unsound. Like Ofra's sister-in-law, Yael, who was so traumatized by boot camp that she was permanently released from the army. She left for New York, escaping the taboo of her breakdown, for a while. It wasn't entirely conscious, however, because at the time I'd pushed the memories of war and rape so far beneath the surface that I genuinely had no idea why I had become so impatient, even volatile, thinking that I was only reacting to Aviv, who had become so moody, melancholy, and withdrawn. And I took it all so personally.

Like our difficulty finding enough privacy at Aviv's parents'. Once, Moshe had opened the sliding glass door to Aviv's bedroom without knocking and found me in my jeans and bra. The door had no lock, and after we moved back into his bedroom from Moshe's library, we'd taken to wedging a sneaker between the door and the wall so that we could have some intimacy and warmth and affection. This had put a strain on us, and now that Aviv had become so distant, I was beginning to feel abandoned. But we didn't explore much of that with Tovah. Instead, we told her about Aviv's fight with his parents, how angry he had become about the wedding invitations, how insulting it was for him to still be treated like a baby when he was about to get married. Aviv would sit in therapy, the poster child of calm, and I would burst out crying.

"Your presence is making this family communicate," Tovah said. "This is good."

Tovah focused on our communication skills, like a good family therapist would, but she never probed too deeply, never asked why I quit the kibbutz or how I'd felt during the war. We went to her every week, faithfully, for more than a month, releasing the pressure that would build each week without ever discovering the root of our troubles. Then Friday night would come, and as usual, Aviv would sit at his desk, face focused on the computer in front of him, retreating into his work like a hermit crab burrowing into the sand.

26

Shalom, Shalom

My mother, father, and sister arrived a week before our reception. Aviv and I picked them up at Ben-Gurion airport in Tel Aviv. My mother's neck and cheeks flushed rose. I wondered what was wrong. "Boy, I'll tell you what, they sure mean business," she said. After landing in Tel Aviv, airport security guards had grilled my mother, father, and sister. They opened their suitcases, nosed around, and wouldn't let my sister through for two hours. Tall, blonde, Nordic people tended to put the Israeli guards on code-red alert.

We stopped at the pancake house on the way to my parents' hotel in Haifa. "This is my favorite place," Aviv said. It looked like the kind of pancake house you'd find off a major highway in the United States. Inside, we sat at a big booth.

Aviv looked over the menu. "I love pancakes," he said.

"Me, too," my mother said.

I tended to worry when Aviv and my mother spoke. The

first time Aviv and I visited my parents in Connecticut, he'd lectured my mother about how to pronounce the guttural *h* in Hebrew. She couldn't get the gargle part of it right, so he'd tell her, "No, that's not it." Big sigh. He also gave her a hard time about New Canaan—Canaan being the biblical name for Israel. "What's this *New* Canaan?" Aviv said, pronouncing it *Ka-NAHN* like an Israeli. We were on a drive, showing Aviv around Fairfield County, our part of Connecticut. "New Canaan is the town next to Stamford," my mother said, pronouncing it *KAY-nun*—the American way. Aviv bristled. "That's not right," he said. "It's *Ka-NAAAAHN*." He dragged out the second syllable for emphasis. My mother warned me about Aviv's "edge." She worried that he might be a "stinker" to me someday, like her own father had been. I told her not to worry, that *sabras* were "prickly on the outside, sweet on the inside." My mother didn't appreciate his thorns.

The waitress took our order, and when it was Aviv's turn, he said, "I'll take pancakes with wiped cream."

My mother cupped her hand over her mouth, giggling into her palm as the waitress scribbled the order on her pad. "It's whipped. *Whipped*, two *p*'s," she said, ribbing him the way she would later rib my Dutch sister-in-law.

Aviv didn't find the humor in it. He had become sensitive about his English, now that he planned to transfer to a school in New York. And my mother's spelling lesson didn't help. Aviv took it out on me that night, the way I'd taken it out on him when Sarah thought that Aviv's old girlfriend was such a lovely girl. And the next day, I blew up at my mother, just like Aviv had at his parents over Ofra's invitations. I started off with "wiped" cream, and I ended up yelling at her for being so insensitive and critical, reminding her of nearly every time she'd ever hurt my feelings, and demanding that she back off. Big time. She did. And, as my mother would say, she learned to "bite her tongue" around Aviv.

My father never said much about Aviv or any other guy I'd ever dated. He wasn't vocal, like my mother. He was the quiet optimist, to a fault sometimes, and she was the voice of reason, otherwise known as worst-case scenarios. My father didn't fit the profile of the Vietnam veteran. He had such a gentle way and only got angry with me once. I was barely five when I snuck out of my bedroom window, climbed into a pin oak, cupped my knees over a branch, and swung upside down—arms dangling toward the front lawn, faded yellow from the Nebraska sun. I wore a cream silk slip that I called my tutu and cowboy boots, my mother's as a girl when she rode Tex, a big, gentle, brown-and-white pinto, on a nearby ranch with Kathy O'Brien—a future national champion cowgirl, who'd sell her parents' 808 acres of tallgrass prairie to the Audubon Society. Neighborhood boys gathered around the oak as I swung upside down wearing my tutu and cowboy boots and nothing else. My father pushed through the front door, marched around the house in his pajamas, and nailed all the screens shut.

After that first row about "wiped" cream, we all got along expertly. The following night, we had a warm and chatty dinner with Moshe and Sarah at a restaurant by the Mediterranean Sea. And then my parents and my sister and Aviv and I traveled for a week, visiting the Baha'i gardens in Haifa, the Crusader city of Akko, the Sea of Galilee, where Jesus recruited fishermen, his disciple Peter's house in Capernaum, the Church of Annunciation in Nazareth, the Roman theater in Caesarea, the Bedouin market in Beersheba.

Summer sun beat on us, beads of sweat on our brows, as we walked through the Old City of Jerusalem, past the Western Wall, up the stairs to the Temple Mount, where the golden Dome of the Rock and slate-gray Al-Aqsa Mosque face each other. Then we took a taxi to the Garden of Gethsemane on the Mount of Olives in the West Bank. My mother told Aviv not to say anything so that no one would hear his Israeli accent, the only thing that would give him away, because as a tall sandy-haired guy in blue jeans and Birkenstock sandals he was often mistaken for a Swede.

The driver chatted with my mother, proudly telling her that he was a Palestinian Christian and that some of the olive trees in the Garden of Gethsemane had been around when Jesus prayed in the garden before his crucifixion. My sister, a photography student at the Corcoran College of Art and Design, took black-and-white photos of the olive trees in the garden, thick trunks and gnarly bark, rough like alligator skin. A photo collage of my sister's olive tree shots in the Garden of Gethsemane still hangs in my parents' finished basement, their family room.

Aviv, our host and tour guide that week, was particularly solicitous of my mother. He knew that she was a Bible reader, so he turned to her and asked, "Do you want see the Church of the Holy Sculpture?"

My mother's eyes lit up. She could barely contain herself, knowing that he'd meant the Church of the Holy Sepulchre.

Somehow, she "bit her tongue," though to this day she will give a good belly laugh at the mention of the Church of the Holy Sculpture—a verbal slip that captured her view of religious icons, as a woman whose faith worships nothing material, and as a woman who knew the actual tomb had been outside of the city. "How about the Pool of Siloam," she said.

I expected Aviv to say something sarcastic, but he smiled, nodded, said that would be fine. He didn't mention that he'd taken me to see that pool on our first trip and how disappointing it might be. He was so courteous to my mother. Aviv hailed a taxi, and we hopped in. The cab nosed down the hill, then slammed on the brakes, and jerked into reverse to avoid children by the roadside, holding stones in their fists. Dust and gravel sprayed like a wave as we backed out of the West Bank. He waited for a while, until the children got out of the way, and then raced back down the hill toward the pool.

We walked into the tunnel and stopped where the water pooled.

"That's it?" my mother said.

"Yep, that's it," I said. I did not know then that if we had waded through the water, we would have reached an ancient reconstruction of the pool at the end of the aqueduct. But the pool from Jesus' time still had not been unearthed.

We got to Masada too late in the afternoon. It was already closed. So we went to the Dead Sea and took a dip in the salty turquoise water, dense as brine. It stung my eyes and skin.

"I'm dying of thirst," my sister said.

"Me, too," my father said.

We tried to order an early dinner, but the kitchen wasn't open yet. The only thing they could offer were drinks and watermelon. We ordered two big plates.

"This is the best watermelon I've ever had," my mother said.

"Me, too," my sister said.

Aviv smiled. He liked to show off his country.

Aviv put his hand on my waist and greeted guests at the reception. "Shalom, shalom, shalom," we said. We rented out the side yard of someone's home. A big white house with a big grassy lawn and an in-ground pool. The family kept their Rottweilers inside during the party. Aviv had wanted to have the reception in an orchard, but renting the yard turned out to be much simpler to pull off. We had a buffet of hors d'oeuvres. Moroccan cigars, stuffed grape leaves, falafel, hummus and pita. I'd picked out peach tablecloths, and Sarah had chosen red carnations as center-pieces. It was a tacky combination of colors, and I wasn't a fan of carnations, either. I preferred roses, but I didn't want to tell Sarah. I didn't want to make a fuss after the trouble over Ofra's invitations. We never used them. Instead, we sent simple cards to about fifty people. Nearly everyone showed up. My mother, father, and sister. Moshe, Sarah, Revital, Ofra and her in-laws. Nadav, his parents, and his brother. All of Sarah's sisters and their families. Even Moshe's sister and her husband with brain cancer— newly arrived Ukrainians, who'd lived near the nuclear wasteland of Chernobyl. Moshe smiled and shook hands with all the guests. Revital, Ofra, and Sarah chatted with my mother and father. Nadav and his brother joked around with my sister, who took photos while Nadav's brother shot the video. Aviv smiled and rested his hand on my waist. I thought that maybe, after all, things would work out in New York.

27
Collateral Damage

Aviv and I flew to New York at the end of July, two days after our reception in Israel. I wanted to fly in on a Tuesday, so that we would arrive just as the *Village Voice* went to press. The weekly paper was on newsstands by Wednesday, and it offered the best deals on apartments back then. I wanted to get a place as soon as possible so we would not regress from the good feeling of that last week in Israel into some other fight about "wiped" cream. That morning I drove my father's Dodge Caravan to the variety store and picked up a copy of the *Voice*. Aviv drove back, and I scanned listings, circling ads for the least expensive studios in Manhattan. At that time, it was still possible to find apartments under a thousand dollars a month in good neighborhoods like the Upper West Side. The New York City real estate market was in a slump, and so was the whole economy—before the Internet and real estate and finance bubbles bloated and burst.

Aviv and I sat at the kitchen table by the picture window. Clumps of hens and chicks, feathery silver mound, white sweet alyssum, mango portulaca, pink astilbe, fuchsia impatiens, purple asters, and sapphire lobelia bloomed in the rock garden below the hemlocks.

"Hey, look at this." I circled an ad in red ink. It was an ad for a studio near the Natural History Museum, a short block from Central Park. Seven hundred dollars a month.

Aviv stared at the ad.

"Not bad," I said.

Aviv shrugged.

"Come on," I said. "We have to get into the city."

We took the Metro-North commuter train into Manhattan that day. Our first errand was at City Hall. We had to get a marriage license because we planned to get married the next day. We had picked the first day of August to marry because it would be so easy to remember. I hesitated before I filled in my name. Aviv and I had had a tiff a few weeks earlier about last names. I had just read Kati Marton's *The Polk Conspiracy*, a book about foreign correspondent George Polk, who was probably murdered because of his investigative reporting on postwar Greece. Marton thanked ABC News anchor Peter Jennings in the acknowledgments. He was her husband at the time. I noted that she had kept her name and asked Aviv what he thought about that.

"What's wrong with my name?" he said

"Nothing's wrong with it," I said. "But if I change my name, how will I explain that I'm the person who wrote all the articles on Latin America and the Middle East?"

Aviv snorted, offended.

It wasn't his name at all. It was the thought of conversations with editors about my byline. I didn't like to mix my personal and professional lives, and the name change would make that impossible. And if I kept both names, every time I wrote a story, I would advertise my marital status. The editor at the *Advocate* didn't even know that I had a fiancé. He thought that I was over in Israel during the Gulf War to study Hebrew on a kibbutz. Period. I thought it through for a week or so, realized that editors would know I was married anyway because of my wedding ring, and reasoned that my children would probably like it better if we all had the same name. I decided to use both. I signed the marriage license, Karol Nielsen Ben-Artzi.

Aviv and I took the subway to the Upper West Side to see the studio. A bleached blonde snapped pink bubblegum and shook our hands. "This place is super cute," she said. She took us up to the third-floor studio. It was compact, but Aviv and I had shared small spaces before, so I didn't think that it would be a problem for us. After all, it was at least twice as big as his bedroom in Israel, and we'd spent seven months there, apart from my five weeks on the kibbutz. Even then, I'd spent weekends in Kiryat Bialik with Aviv.

"Great floors," I said.

The wood floors had a new finish, dark brown and shiny. The studio had two large closets, overhead storage, a small kitchen alcove, and windows that overlooked Columbus Avenue. Restaurants and boutiques ran along that strip, the Upper West Side's Madison Avenue. We had a view of the Natural History Museum, a red stone fortress across the street. And we were a block away from Central Park. It was one of the best neighborhoods in Manhattan. The studio was renovated, clean, the right price. I wanted it bad.

The agent blew a bubble. It snapped. "So you'll take it?"

I looked at Aviv. He hovered near the door, pale and gaunt, like a prisoner of war.

"We'll take it," I said.

She said that I had to put down a two-hundred-dollar deposit to hold the apartment. She knew of an automatic teller machine across the street. I said that was fine, though I wondered if I had enough money left in my overdraft account to cover the deposit. We had received several thousand dollars in wedding gifts at the Israeli reception, and Moshe had given Aviv his education savings. Ten thousand shekels converted to more than eight thousand dollars—about two thousand dollars less than Aviv had hoped. We hadn't had time to deposit any of that, but I didn't let on. The agent led us to the ATM, and I inserted my card. We were outside Isabella's, an Italian restaurant with a sidewalk café. I had gone there the night I moved into my first Manhattan apartment. It had only been two years since then, but it felt as remote as my childhood. The ATM machine spit out a stack of twenties, and I handed them to the agent. She scratched out a receipt.

"Great," she said. Snapped a bubble. She said that we could sign the lease once she did a credit check on me. She said that Aviv's credit history wouldn't matter: he didn't have one in the United States. She caught a cab downtown.

Aviv stood on the corner, fists clenched. "You don't ask me what I think," he said.

"I didn't want you to spoil it," I said. I knew from experience that affordable apartments in good neighborhoods only stayed on the market for a few hours. I knew we had to put down a deposit right then. Aviv wouldn't speak to me on the train ride home.

That evening, we lay on my bed and watched the news. Leonard Jeffries was on, ranting about the Jews, the mafia, and their racist "conspiracy" in Hollywood. At that time, Jeffries was a professor at City College, where Aviv would begin studying in a few weeks. Aviv and I stared at the television, stunned. It brought me back to those nights in Israel when we'd watched white police officers from Los Angeles beat black motorist Rodney King, who famously pleaded, "Can we all get along?" Aviv and I would watch the news in silence, waiting for the NBA finals to come on. Lakers versus Bulls. Magic Johnson, Michael Jordan, head to head. Aviv liked the Bulls because of their coach, Phil Jackson. Aviv said that he was the most intelligent coach in the NBA. Aviv respected that. I liked the Bulls because of Michael Jordan. I'd watch him jump and twirl, dunk balls into the basket, and lob three-pointers across the court, acrobatic and graceful as a ballet dancer. Now the NBA finals were over, and all we had was Leonard Jeffries, bursting our belief that New York was a place we'd find peace.

Aviv didn't kiss me good morning. He rolled out of bed, took a shower, put on his dress slacks. Summer-weight wool in pale mustard. We'd picked them up a few months back at a mall in Haifa for the reception in Israel. Now they hung loosely and low on his hips. Aviv had wasted away from sinewy buck to an emaciated survivor of war. He stared out of the window on the ride into New York. We wound up the hill, along my childhood running route, passing maple, beech, oak, and tulip trees. My father drove. My mother sat with her hands in her lap, and for the first time that I could remember, she didn't comment on my father's driving. My father never had an accident, but he wasn't the most cautious driver. When I was a teenager, we took a family trip to California and drove from Los Angeles to San Francisco along the coastal highway, a single lane in each direction along steep, curvy cliffs. My father raced along the cliffs, moving into the oncoming traffic lane to pass cars ahead of him. We'd stop at an observation deck. The cars he'd passed would zip by. But he'd overtake them once we got back on the road. Most of the time, though, my mother was the only one who noticed his infractions, like his latest technique of holding a cell phone in one hand and gesturing with his other, leaving no hands for the steering wheel. But that day, my mother didn't mention his driving. She was quiet. We all were. Aviv, me, my mother, father, and sister. She was our witness. It was our wedding day.

My father parked in lower Manhattan, and we walked over to the New York City Clerk's Office. My mother stopped us in the cobblestone courtyard. She turned to Aviv. The color had drained from his face.

"Sweetie, you look a little shaky," my mother said to Aviv. "How 'bout a pretzel?" She pointed to the pretzel vendor in the courtyard.

Aviv shook his head. "No, I'm not hungry," he said.

"But sweetie, you look like you're going to faint," she said.

"Okay," he said.

My mother and Aviv went over to the pretzel vendor.

He came back with a Pepsi and a big pretzel. He bit into the pretzel, took a sip of Pepsi.

"Better?" my mother said.

Aviv nodded.

We went inside and headed down a long corridor that had the look of an inner-city school in need of renovation. We found the waiting area and sat on metal folding chairs as a woman leafed through papers behind a steel desk in the corner. It felt like a classroom. She was the teacher. We were her students, waiting quietly for class to begin. For a while we were the only ones in the room. Then a young Latino couple came in. The girl wore a white wedding gown, sequins on the bust. The groom wore a black tux. A man called out, "Ben-Artzi."

The clerk led us into a small room, almost as small as the sealed room where we'd dodged missiles. Gray walls and gray carpet. No flowers, music, or wedding guests. The clerk went to the podium and waved Aviv and me toward him. My parents stayed along the wall, and my sister moved next to my side. She wore a pink cotton shift, something you'd wear as a guest at a wedding in Connecticut. I had on the same kind of dress. My mother had lowered the neckline on the bridesmaid dress I'd worn for my friend Erin's wedding, soon after coming home from Argentina. She was a driven scholar and athlete—like my high school friend Sarah—who'd been captain of the Penn women's crew team and married a rower from Princeton in a pretty chapel in Southern California. I didn't have any bridesmaids, only my sister standing beside us as our witness. Aviv didn't smile. He stood like a guard at Buckingham Palace.

"Are you Karol Nielsen and Aviv Ben-Artzi?"

"Yes," we answered together, glancing at each other.

The clerk went right to the vows. We had no prepared readings, nothing religious, no God or philosopher or leader of men blessing us that day. It only took a few seconds to say, "I do." Now I was wearing a ring, a thin gold band we'd picked up for seventy shekels in downtown Tel Aviv.

"You may kiss the bride," he said.

We kissed and embraced, rocking in each other's arms. Maybe, just maybe, the war was over.

My father took us to the real estate agency, and we signed the lease. Aviv didn't make a fuss about the apartment, though I could tell that he was still upset. He'd been so distant all day. That night, Aviv and I stayed in my childhood bedroom in Connecticut. The room had a big window that faced the backyard, thick woods on either side of a big lawn that sloped like a golf course down to a pond that everyone called "the lake." Canada geese squawked and waddled around the lawn, fertilizing it with digested grass. There used to be a cluster of birch trees in the rock garden in the middle of the yard. My mother sent my brother, a teenager at the time, to cut down one that had rotted. He came back in the house and said, "I cut down the birch trees for ya, Mom." Now fieldstones circle a lone Japanese maple, a fireball in the middle of the yard.

In the dark, I could see a few specks of light coming from the home across the pond, hidden behind thick woods. Cicadas sang loudly, searching for love. I slipped on a T-shirt and got under the white quilt. Aviv sat on the other side of the bed in his underwear. He bent over and pulled off his socks. His back still to me, he twisted around and slid under the covers. He lay on his side, looking away from me out of the dark window. My heart beat fast, like it does on a quick-paced run. I wanted him to turn over, kiss me, and caress me. I waited. There was only silence, no movement. He lay turned away, curled up on his side, ribs poking at the quilt, not touching me.

Aviv called Con Edison in the morning to turn on the electricity in the new apartment. He looked through his backpack, pulled out his passport, gave her the number. He slumped on the edge of the bed, his face like snow. He handed me the phone.

"What is it?" I said.

"She wants a big deposit because I'm a foreigner," he said.

I gave the woman my details, and she apologized but repeated, "It's just that he's a foreigner. He doesn't have a history with us." I called the phone company, too, and got our service turned on. Aviv sat on the bed and stared out of the window at the dogwoods.

We had a wedding reception at my parents' home in Connecticut. A steel drum band played in the backyard, set up with tables under a tent. My mother invited my aunts, uncles, cousins, her friends and mine. We had a buffet of roast beef and sole and a three-tiered wedding cake. Chocolate with vanilla icing. Aviv cut the cake, and we fed each other a piece. Aviv put his hand around my waist and kissed me. Everyone said, "Ah," and clapped. We sealed the top layer of our wedding cake in a plastic container, brought it back to New York, and put it in the freezer. I wanted to follow tradition and eat the cake on our first anniversary.

We moved into the city, and within weeks the Crown Heights riot broke out. A Lubavitcher driver had hit and killed a young black boy. Three days of rioting followed. Looting, anti-Semitic hollering, a fatal stabbing of a rabbinical student. A pogrom in Brooklyn. I clipped stories in the newspaper about the riot, Leonard Jeffries, David Duke. A former Ku Klux Klan grand wizard running for president of the United States. We had an open reporting assignment during my first week at the Columbia University School of Journalism, and I knew right away that I had to go to Crown Heights and write about the riot. I had a sense of urgency. I had to understand. For me and Aviv and our children. I would write my thesis about it, reading books and talking to experts like Jim Sleeper and Charles Hamilton. So obsessive that sometime during the middle of the year, Aviv would once say, "Do we have to talk about that?"

On the long subway ride to Brooklyn, I thought of the boy who died so young and the rabbinical student who was stabbed to death during the riot. It seemed so tragic, all around. Down in Crown Heights, police stood guard in full riot gear along the strangely quiet streets. I expected to sense the rage, a friction that might ignite any minute. But I couldn't feel the heat. I walked down President Street, where the accident had happened. A shrine of carnations and votive candles nestled against a cinderblock wall. Painted red. Rusty red, like too-ripe tomatoes. A long poem hung on the wall above the shrine. An angry, anti-Semitic poem. I copied the words into my notebook, quickly, and stuffed it back into my blazer pocket. I didn't want to get beat up, like the *Village Voice* photographer. I walked down the street about a block. An Orthodox Jewish father helped his little son pedal his bike. It tipped, and the father's hand steadied it. Seemed like the training wheels had just come off. Then I went back to the diner across from the accident scene. A West Indian place serving rice and beans and strong coffee. I ordered a cup and asked the man if he'd seen the accident. I didn't take out my notebook.

"I see everything," he said, in a lovely, lilting voice. "The car goes too fast, man, too fast, hits that boy, pins him to the wall, the wall of his own home." He shook his ebony dreadlocks. "They always driving fast, passing through red lights, the police leading the way." He meant the Lubavitcher motorcade that passed every week to visit the gravesite of their spiritual leader, buried in Queens.

I thanked him, paid for my coffee, and walked to Utica Avenue. I stopped at a Jewish bakery, bought a bagel, and eavesdropped a bit. Nothing about the riot. Life went on, the way it did in Israel during the Gulf War. People went out carrying gas masks like shoulder bags, driving around, parking cars, walking, shopping, sipping cappuccino, and eating cheesecake like Aviv and me.

Things should have been good between us. Aviv got into the master's program at City College within a semester, and I was doing well in school, too. But things were not good like we hoped they would be in New York. Aviv withdrew to schoolwork, like he had in Israel after the war. Weekends would come, and he'd sit at his computer. I'd complain, and then we'd see a movie or go for cheesecake and cappuccino. Aviv didn't make friends at school, and when I got invitations, he rarely wanted to go. Even when he did, he had no enthusiasm. Like the time that he sat in front of the television watching an NBA game before a friend's art opening. He was in his underwear on the couch. He hadn't even showered.

I lashed out. "We have to be there in twenty minutes, get your butt off the couch."

What had happened to the Aviv who couldn't sleep nights in Manhattan because of the things he'd miss if he did? The Aviv who hiked with me in Peru? The Aviv who took me to SOB's, the Blue Note, B. B. King live on a Hudson River pier? The Aviv who was always up for a walk through the city, cheesecake and cappuccino, dinner and a movie? Where was that Aviv? He'd promised me that we would be okay in New York, that we'd be happy like we were before. But we weren't. Aviv parceled out affection like rations in a depression.

I starved.

I had lost patience for the recluse he'd become. I had no elasticity left and blamed Aviv for everything that went wrong. My mother upgraded the software on my computer while I was in Israel, and somehow she misplaced all my files from that hard drive. I never put anything on diskettes, so everything that I'd ever written on that computer was missing, including volumes of journal entries during my year in Argentina. The diskettes containing my files turned up later. She'd sent them to my brother by mistake. But that day, I ripped into my mother, and when I got off the phone with her, Aviv asked, "Don't you have a back-up?" His question was like gasoline on a campfire. I blew.

Another night, Aviv kept me up coughing, and I complained. "I need to sleep, God damn it, I'm in graduate school." I had a long day ahead of me and didn't want go into it exhausted. So Aviv got up and coughed in the bathroom, for hours. Once, when he came home and asked how I was, I told him, "I was good until you got home." I wasn't trying to be cruel. I was stating a frustrating fact. I even took it out on Aviv when Woody Allen left Mia Farrow for her adopted daughter, Soon Yi Previn. We liked Woody Allen films and looked to Woody and Mia as a kind of interfaith role model. So naturally, we went to see his latest film, *Husbands and Wives*, a bleak portrait of unhappy marriages. Aviv said that it was a poignant and honest film.

"How can you say that?" I said. "I want more out of marriage than that."

The school year ended in May, and a few weeks later, I ran into a classmate. She said she had found a job as a writer for the *Advocate,* my hometown newspaper in Connecticut. I told her I hadn't found anything yet because I wanted to stay in New York, the most competitive place to find a job in journalism.

"Oh, that's right, you have to stay here," she said. "You're married."

It wasn't the first time that journalists had made digs about marriage. A female professor bragged that she didn't have any "baggage like a husband or children." And a male professor said during class that "marriage ruins writing careers." I was the only one wearing a wedding ring.

I pulled out my Newport Lights and paced along Broadway. That night, I told Aviv about what my classmate had said, how it hurt and made me want to smoke. I told him I was addicted.

"You're not addicted," he said.

"I am," I said.

I told him I smoked every day, needed to because everything hurt.

"What is hurting?"

So I told him what hurt. Every single thing, going on so long that we missed the NBA game at Madison Square Garden. New York Knicks versus the Chicago Bulls, allowing Aviv only one opening.

"You never do my laundry," he said.

And it was true, I didn't do his laundry, the way his mother always had. I didn't cook for him, either. I thought of us as equals, as friends.

When I was done, Aviv looked exhausted. "You throw everything at me like this is the last fight we are going to have," he said.

"I can't take it anymore, I'm leaving," I said.

Aviv held my arms, tears dripping down his cheeks. "But I love you, please don't go, please don't go."

Aviv always told me he loved me, and I believed him. I loved him, too, and told him so all the time. But we had lost the ability to show that love. Aviv said we should try therapy again. I didn't have much faith. We'd gone to Tovah once a week for the last few months in Israel, and the only thing she'd ever said to us was how good it was that Aviv was communicating with his family, for once. I hadn't gone to her to help Aviv communicate with his family. I'd gone to her to save my relationship with Aviv. I still loved him.

And that's why I stayed.

Aviv and I went to see someone Aviv's professor recommended. We waited in the reception area until she opened the door to her office. She smiled, a slender brunette. She reminded me of Amit, Aviv's girlfriend from high school. It wasn't a good association.

"Come in," she said.

She sat down in a big leather chair, and we took the couch. She was professional, put together, serious. She looked like the kind of psychologist who would study her patients and write best-selling books about their traumas. She took out a yellow legal-sized notepad. "Before we get started, let me get some facts straight. You're from Israel, right?"

"Yes, that's right," Aviv said.

She told him that she'd spent some time in Israel, switched to Hebrew, and chatted for a few minutes about the clinic she'd worked at there and how much she liked his country. Then she turned to me and asked me about my background. I told her that I grew up in Connecticut, that I was raised as a Christian Scientist.

"An Israeli and a Christian Scientist, it's amazing that you've made it this far," she said.

She didn't hear us when we said that that we didn't fight about that. We still worked those problems out, like the time Aviv was down about Hanukkah. "I rely on my family to celebrate," he said. "I realize I don't know what to do." So we got a book about Hanukkah at the Judaica store, bought a menorah, and lit candles every night. About that time, my parents were going to Colorado to ski over Christmas, and my father stopped by the software store where Aviv worked as a salesman to drop off our Christmas presents, unannounced. I went ballistic and told my father that he should have checked with me first, before delivering our gifts. I didn't want Christmas to overshadow Hanukkah, after all the effort we'd made. And I comforted Aviv when Ofra's brother-in-law called from New Jersey, where he was a student at Princeton, and gave Aviv a hard time about his politics. "I told him I'm for Clinton, and he said that every good Israeli should be for Bush, but that is not the worst part, I am forgetting words in Hebrew." I knew we would have challenges because of our differences, but those were the things we handled with care. We saw each other's humanity first and foremost, a shared vision that was still the cement of our relationship. And the easy assumption that the divide of language and culture and religion was the solitary root of our troubles clouded our case with confusion.

We went to another therapist, my pick. I'd met her on a story assignment for the journalism school's newspaper, and she agreed to meet with us. Angela was big and warm, like a grandmother. I liked her and hoped she could help. We told her our story, how we still loved each other, but Aviv withheld affection, and I blew up. Aviv was calm, like always, and I bawled and bawled. Angela suggested that I see her alone. I'd cry and tell her how much I loved him but how much it all hurt.

"What hurts?" she said.

"Everything," I said.

I told her that I missed the affection we'd shared in the beginning, that I didn't have patience for who we had become, that I wanted to leave. Living like that hurt too much.

"Maybe you were only meant to be friends," she said.

I wept so hard I quivered.

When Aviv and I saw Angela together, he was always

composed, like a wise professor. "How can you sit there so calmly after all we've been through? You make me look like a basket case," I'd say when we got home. He'd sit and sulk in silence, even though he never sulked in front of Angela. Ever. Then one day, after another long argument about the same thing—his withdrawal, my impatience—he told me the truth. "Israel has done this to us, and if I let myself feel everything I will break down," he said. He lay on the bed, put his hands over his eyes, and wept. By now, I had suppressed so much of what happened in Israel that it felt like an excuse when Aviv blamed his country for our problems, almost a year after moving to New York. Aviv never told Angela how he felt. Neither of us did. It wasn't a conscious thing, but looking back, it's clear to me that we withheld the most vital parts of our story first from Tovah and now Angela.

And we could not escape our dangerous pattern. He would withdraw affection, and I'd explode, threaten to leave. He'd cry, plead for me to stay, and I'd agree. Then we'd make up, share warmth and I love you's all night. I'd feel better after the fights, but Aviv said that it would take him days, even weeks, to recover. He'd retreat into himself, and soon enough, I'd blow up, and it would start over. Again and again and again. I couldn't stand who we had become and felt that we were to blame. Aviv didn't agree, blaming the "the pressure cooker" that made him dream about the kind of peace he'd find on a sheep farm in New Zealand.

A knock in the middle of the night. "Fire, fire," he said. It was a fireman. Our building was on fire. Aviv and I put on clothes and climbed out of the window, down the fire escape. My pants caught on the ladder. It ripped the fabric at my hip. Aviv and I stood across the street by the Natural History Museum. The roof sparked. Flames shot along the electrical wiring, zipping along the roof like a lit fuse. Fireworks on our roof. I asked the fire marshal what went down.

"Accelerant on the wiring in the basement," he said. "That's all I know."

A film of black soot coated everything, our computers, laser printer, fax, butcher-block desk, and white down comforter. Everything. The building had gone into receivership and the court-appointed agent sent us a new lease. It didn't include the security deposit that we'd paid to move in. We complained, but the agent didn't fix the lease. Aviv said that we should move. A bigger place would do us good. Maybe we wouldn't fight as much. I hunted through ads, and this time I found a one-bedroom for $790 fifteen blocks uptown. We took it that day, even though I wasn't crazy about it. The molding and walls were lumpy from too many coats of paint, and the blond floors had lost their shine. But it was bigger. And we had a bedroom. We could close the door and sleep, if one of us wanted to stay up late, take a nap, have some privacy. It didn't take long for me to regret the larger space. Maybe we fought less. But it widened the distance between us.

I began to miss the nights during graduate school when we'd meet at the diner after my shift at the broadcast-news clip service, a job that was a curiosity since so few of the students worked during graduate school, a full-time job for us. When I contacted my thesis advisor about ten years later to ask for advice, he said, "Of course I remember you. You were the one who worked." We would meet up at midnight like secret lovers and talk and laugh and smile at each other, holding hands over a cup of soup and grilled cheese sandwiches. But school was over, and the pressure of performing had ended, and finally we fell apart.

Aviv said that we should go on a honeymoon. He did all the research, told me that the Cayman Islands had the best snorkeling in the Caribbean.

"As good as Eilat?" I said.

"That good," he said.

He booked the flight, made the hotel reservations, planned the whole thing.

The first night at the hotel, Aviv said he was tired, that he needed to get some sleep. He was in bed by 9 p.m.

In the morning, we lay on the beach, reading books.

"Do you want to snorkel?" I said.

"Later," he said.

It felt like we were retirees, going to bed early, laying about with our books.

Aviv rented some fins that afternoon, but the water was murky. I couldn't see a thing. Aviv said that it would probably be better in the submarine. So we took a submarine ride through the coral reef. The water was gray, and so were the fish. It wasn't like Eilat at all. That night, we went to the grocery store, bought peanut butter, crackers, and cheese for dinner. It was so expensive in the Caymans that we only ate out once. After a few days, Aviv said that he missed New York, couldn't wait to get back to his routine. He went to sleep early. Every night.

I opened the freezer and took out the chocolate cake. I set it down on the kitchen table.

"Why you don't say something?" Aviv said.

"How could you forget?" I sobbed.

Aviv stared at the cake, shoulders slumped.

"Say something," I said.

"Sorry," he said.

"You miss our anniversary. That's all you can say?"

His eyes welled with tears. "I'm sorry," he said.

I didn't leave him that day, but another day, months later, when Aviv rolled out of bed without giving me a kiss, a hug, or even a smile. He had built a fortress around himself, and fighting was the only way I could break in. I was tired of fighting.

I went to the living room and found Aviv at the computer.

"You promised we'd be happy in New York, like we were in the beginning. But you're so different. You're nothing like the guy I met in Peru."

"That was vacation," he said. His tone had turned cold, hard, dismissive.

I didn't pack a bag. I picked up my wallet and keys and caught a train to Connecticut. A woman sat next to me. Pulled out her knitting. A baby sweater. Light blue. Her brown finger looped yarn over the needles, over and over. Tears spilled down my cheeks. The woman peered at me through thick glasses. I looked away from her and stared out the window, as the train rolled past burned-out buildings in Harlem toward sailboats in the Long Island Sound.

28
Homecoming

At first, I'd just wanted some sleep, some time to sort through my feelings, but I soon found that it was far easier to move on. I only stayed with my parents for a few weeks before moving to my own place and finding a job as the managing editor of a weekly newspaper in the Bronx, soon becoming a stringer for the *New York Times* and a freelance writer for *New York Newsday*. I covered the hard and the soft. Murders, rapes, drugs, gangs, topless bars, homeless shelters, crumbling schools, community gardens, filmmakers, authors, actors, activists. Like the one I called the Lone Ranger of graffiti removal.

I smoked a pack a day before long. Like police officers and firefighters. Focusing me like strong coffee, soothing me like red wine. But now and then, something would catch me off guard, like the time I covered a protest in the southeast Bronx after drug dealers had vandalized a Catholic church. Afterwards, I listened to mass and began to weep. A young man sat down beside me and invited me to a prayer group. I didn't go, knowing I would have to explain my tears but would only be able to say what I'd said to Angela when she'd asked, "What hurts?" And I'd said, "Everything."

I went to my own church instead, thinking that maybe all of this had happened because I'd fallen away from my faith and prayer and God. I didn't drink much, and never would, but I used the occasional beer, a glass or two of red wine, and mostly cigarettes as a way to relax me like running always did. But I hadn't run much during graduate school, reporting and writing all day and working nights at the broadcast-news clip service, and by the time I tried again my pack-a-day habit had such a devastating effect on my performance that I felt winded after only a mile. I tried to quit several times, smoking more each time I'd go back, until I finally called a Christian Science practitioner who'd been a smoker, too. "Dear, you just need to handle the thought of temptation," she said. This time the urge simply fell away from me and never returned.

Aviv and I kept seeing Angela, separately, and several months after I'd left she said, "All he does is talk about you." I knew he still loved me, but I could not understand how we had come to this. Why had I become so excitable? Aviv so melancholy? Angela suggested I cut down on caffeine, encouraged Aviv to eat red meat. It was a Band Aid, and we needed a tourniquet. Angela was the best of the three therapists we'd seen, mostly because she cared about both of us and hoped that we would work it out, but despite all of her compassionate counsel, we would divorce in four years and never live together again.

A year after our divorce, I ran into Aviv on the street as I was leaving my apartment near Lincoln Center. He was holding a thick book by Taylor Branch, who'd won the Pulitzer Prize for his chronicle of the American Civil Rights movement, *Parting the Waters: America in the King Years, 1954–1963*. Aviv had bought the book at the big bookstore near me and was on his way home, about forty blocks up Broadway from me. He'd never left New York, staying to finish his PhD and later to work as a professor. We had a long, long talk while wandering through the park on that warm fall day. Aviv said I looked good and wanted to know if I was seeing anyone. I told him I'd just broken up with an artist who lived in my building, a tall and buff and funny man who used to call me Wounded Sparrow. We were at a wedding on Long Island when word spread around our table that Israeli prime minister Yitzhak Rabin had been shot. Assassinated by a fanatic for making peace with the Palestinians, like Egyptian president Anwar Sadat had been for making peace with Israel.

The artist was an Irish Catholic who took me on motorcycle adventures and cooked like a chef, but we'd butt heads over his often insensitive humor, and I'd lose patience with him, too. I told Aviv that the first time I met his mother, she said, "The Protestants, hateful people." She had grown up in Ireland, and I would come to adore her warmth and grit and good cooking, but I took it hard, at first. It was just the three of us at their small little dining table in the kitchen, and my boyfriend kept eating his mashed potatoes without another thought.

Aviv laughed. "Me, I'm seeing an African American

woman, and so eventually she wants to marry. But I think maybe I am not ready, so we break up, and then Revital starts asking, 'So, have you seen Karol?'" Aviv sighed and said, "We had all the problems a couple could have except race."

We laughed at the absurdity of it all, by this time sitting on the steps near Juilliard, after talking and walking and exploring for hours, like we used to do.

"I think I need someone who believes in God," I said, believing that faith was the antidote.

Aviv bristled. "So you are saying our parents were right?"

Aviv had taken my mother's jokes and early judgments as evidence of her disapproval, but she never thought that our mixed marriage was a problem for us, seeing us instead as a young and idealistic couple who fiercely defended each other, as if it were Aviv and me against the world.

"No, I just want someone more like me," I said, though I would find that I was still drawn to people who questioned, like Aviv. "Do you think we'd have made it without the war?" It was a question that was never far from my consciousness but somehow felt so elusive and mysterious and ineffable.

Aviv thought for a moment and said, "No, I think the war showed us our differences in the beginning. I think we would have split anyway."

It felt like he'd stabbed me in the gut, even though I'd just told him that I didn't want someone like him who didn't believe in God. "What are our differences?" I said.

"You are an optimist, and I am a pessimist. This is because I am an atheist, and to me that means to doubt."

Both of us were trying to move forward, and sometimes the easiest way was to take cover in reductive certainty.

I used to cry whenever people would ask, "What happened?" Always groping for the right words to explain how things had fallen apart. Invariably, people who were Jewish would say, "But why didn't you stay in Israel?" And those who weren't would say, "But why did you go to Israel?" Conversations always left me feeling drained and lonely and raw as I'd try to process the sundry speculations. Some blamed Aviv: "He was hostile." "He only loved himself." "He just wanted a green card." Others blamed me: "You beat the life out of him," the artist once said. At first, I mostly blamed myself or Aviv, too, but I knew that it was far more complicated.

I told Angela that I wanted to write about Aviv and me, to tell our story. She smiled and gently said, "You are too young, you don't have anything to say." I would do it anyway, knowing intuitively that if I could piece all the facts together like a dogged detective, I could eventually solve our case. When I finished, I showed it to friends and family and anyone who asked.

"This is a great story," said Josh, my pessimistic Jewish atheist friend. He was a movie critic and a foreign and independent film buff who would normally mumble or grunt or go silent when friends shared their screenplays with him. He told me how his sister had married an Israeli, how they lived in Israel for a while, and how her husband's family only spoke Hebrew with her. She struggled with the language and the toughness of Israeli culture like I had, so they moved to California. Josh didn't think stories needed to have a message; it was enough to render an authentic experience.

Others searched for meaning. "What are you saying?" my mother said. I had no grand message back then, beyond look at what we endured, look how it broke us. "This is like *Schindler's List*," the artist said. But so many assumed that our mixed marriage was to blame that it had a brainwashing effect: "How could you marry an atheist?" "This is what happens when you are not true to yourself." "You always feel an undercurrent of disapproval in a mixed marriage."

Then I shared it with Terry, a PhD psychologist who was hidden in a convent in Poland during the Holocaust. "Being married to a depressed person is very difficult," she said. Her first husband was a Holocaust survivor, too, and he never let go of his survivor's guilt. I felt a weight lifting off of me, for the first time forgiving myself for leaving Aviv, so afraid that he'd sink deeper into depression after I was gone that I called my mother. "Put him in the ark," she said, reminding me of how Moses's mother had put him in the ark, letting him float through the rushes. Safe, secure. I reworked the book and showed it to her.

"I think it was the war," she said, suggesting that I elaborate on why the war was so lonely for me.

"Everyone knows that war is lonely," I said.

"No, I don't think they do."

I set the story aside for several years, feeling overwhelmed after the September 11 attacks and then the wars in Afghanistan and Iraq, these new wars making me feel like I was reliving my own. I channeled my stress into sports, like I did when Sarah died, finishing my first Ironman triathlon six months after the invasion of Iraq. It was an easy course in Panama City, Florida, but the 140.6 miles of swimming and biking and running took me nearly seventeen hours to cover, crossing the finish line fifteen minutes before the midnight cutoff, unlike the fastest triathletes, who can finish in half that time. It wasn't about speed, for me. It was a very conscious metaphor for life. Telling myself over and over again, *If I can get through this long and brutal and humiliating and strangely exhilarating race, I can get through this long and brutal and humiliating and strangely exhilarating thing called life.*

When I dug back into my story, reading books and articles and documents to help me find the words for what I felt, I discovered the leading traumatic stress expert Edna Foa, an Israeli behavioral psychologist at the University of Pennsylvania who has survivors of war, terrorism, rape, and other traumas tell and retell their stories so that the events lose their power to traumatize—something my father had done when he came home from Vietnam—and then she has them face the source of their wounds. For me, that meant researching the war and its aftershock. And as I dug, I discovered that traumatic stress can lead to flashbacks, hypervigilance, nightmares, insomnia, irritability, aggression, depression, withdrawal. Other life stresses make people all the more vulnerable. And in turn these patterns can lead to breakups, drug and alcohol dependence, unemployment, suicide. I wasn't up for talking to therapists anymore, but I kept going back to the story, wrestling with it the way Jacob wrestled with the angel until it blessed him. And when I was done, it was as if I'd finally come home after a long, long journey, sorrow sweeping over me as I wondered, What would have happened to Aviv and me if only we'd known?

Once, when Aviv and I were still together, Angela asked, "Do you think this has anything to do with the war?" Aviv turned to me, and we began laughing, uncontrollably, like we had in the sealed room, when we realized that the beads on my gas mask were condensed breath instead of chemical warfare. At the time, I thought, The war? Where do we begin with the war? I could see us running to the sealed room, putting on our gas masks, waiting for the air raid to end. But by now, it almost seemed like a weird prank, since none of the Scuds contained any kind of poison, and none of them managed to strike anything strategic like Israel's nuclear reactor or its refineries, despite many tries. On the first night of air raids, two of the Scuds exploded near the refineries in Haifa Bay. One damaged stores and apartment buildings, but nobody was killed, and the other plunged into the Lev Ha'Mifratz Shopping Mall under construction by the port. When it opened, Aviv and I went to the mall and chuckled as we looked up at the Scud mobile, hanging from the atrium.

Angela only asked about the war once, and we never answered her question, apart from our laughter. Even if she had asked again, I couldn't have answered her question back then, the memory of the war having slipped so far from conscious memory that it felt like staring into total blackness when I finally began to write, patching the scattered memories together like a jigsaw puzzle, remembering some small piece that would connect with another until all of the memories fit. But now, I think of the siren's slow and relentless beat as our finale—a sad, sad song about war and the unraveling of Aviv and me. I see how war and terror squander innocence and twist the soul, even if you are not among the visibly wounded or dead. It was as if we had never left that room, had never taken off those masks, had never returned to our old selves. We were black elephants, still.

Acknowledgments

I'm forever grateful for Editor in Chief Heather Lundine, Assistant Editor Bridget Barry, and Project Editor Joeth Zucco at the University of Nebraska Press, as well as memoir writers Sonya Huber, Kaylie Jones, and Michael Soussan, who wrote moving and deeply meaningful blurbs about my memoir. I want to thank literary magazine editors Willard Cook, Jamison Klagmann, Robert Lewis, Mira Placin, and my mentor Adam Sexton for publishing parts of this memoir; Robert Atwan, the series editor of *The Best American Essays*, for naming excerpts as notable essays of the year; Noa Greenberg for her careful review of the Hebrew transliterations; Koa Beck for an insightful interview about this book in the *Daily Brink*, Alan Terker and Stephanie Schorow for publishing my stories about Latin America and the Middle East on the op-ed page of the *Advocate* of Stamford, Connecticut; and William Black, Theresa Cahn-Tober, Betty Christiansen, Vivian Eyre, Sorche Fairbank, Paul Ferrari, Peter Golder, Maria Elena Gonzalez,

Sonya Huber, Ira Israel, Mary V. Lauro, Liz Jones, Martha Mortenson, Noranne Nielsen, Josh Ralske, Melle Randall, Caroline Schechter, Adam Sexton, Jim Smith, Kimberly Feltes Taylor, Walteen Grady Truely, my parents, and others for offering insightful feedback on my manuscript. I'd like to thank my professors at the Columbia University School of Journalism Samuel G. Freedman and Dale Maharidge; my high school English teacher Jerry McWilliams, who had his class keep a journal; Alex Steele and the staff at the Gotham Writers' Workshop and New York University who hired me to teach; the Writers Room and its many talented members; and all the writers, editors, students, friends, family, and publishing professionals behind me and this book, especially *Guernica* editors Michael Archer, Rebecca Bates, and Joel Whitney, who published my essay about the journey from journalist to writer and poet; *Smith Magazine*'s editor, Larry Smith, who chose my war-themed essay and poem for his Harper Perennial anthology, *The Moment*; University of Nebraska Press director Donna Shear, Publicity Manager Cara Pesek, and Senior Designer Andrea Shahan, who created my book jacket; my graduate school classmate Christian Moerk, who shared advice and his ear; my sister, Cynthia Nielsen, who took my author photos; my nephew, Aidan Wyatt Pensiero, who brings an abundance of joy to my life; and my mother and father, who loved and supported and believed in me during all the years it took me to get here.

"Litmus Test" first appeared in *Epiphany* and was named a notable essay in *The Best American Essays*.

"The New Zealand Sheep Farmer and the Recruit" first

appeared in *Lumina* and was named a notable essay in *The Best American Essays*.

"Nine-Point-Two Miles" first appeared in *North Dakota Quarterly*.

"Sabra" first appeared in *Permafrost*.

Selected Bibliography

For the Israeli experience during the first Gulf War, I relied on my recollections—corroborated by my calendar and my articles for the *Advocate* of Stamford, Connecticut, as well as those in the archives of the *Jerusalem Post* and other publications; the Massachusetts Institute of Technology Defense and Arms Control Studies Program's working paper "Casualties and Damage from Scud Attacks in the 1991 Gulf War"; Human Rights Watch's report "Needless Deaths in the Gulf War: Civilian Casualties during the Air Campaign and Violations of the Laws of War"; and other sources. For the broader experience of the Gulf War, including its context and aftermath, I relied on Rick Atkinson's *Crusade: The Untold Story of the Persian Gulf War*; Micah L. Sifry and Christopher Cerf's *The Gulf War Reader: History, Documents, Opinions*; Seymour Hersh's *Against All Enemies: Gulf War Syndrome: The War between America's Ailing Veterans and Their Government*; Joost Hiltermann's *A Poisonous Affair: America, Iraq, and the Gassing of Halab-*

ja; Scott Ritter's *Iraq Confidential: The Untold Story of the Intelligence Conspiracy to Undermine the* UN *and Overthrow Saddam Hussein*; Kenneth Timmerman's *The Death Lobby: How the West Armed Iraq*; a 1999 United Nations Special Commission report summing up weapons inspections in Iraq following the Gulf War; and others.

The U.S. Department of Health and Human Services Centers for Disease Control offered facts about chemical and biological agents including anthrax, botulinum toxin, mustard gas, sarin, tabun, and vx. The U.S. Department of Veterans Affairs provided information about traumatic stress, and its treatment is well-rendered in Jerome Groopman's article for the *New Yorker,* "The Grief Industry: How Much Does Crisis Counseling Help—or Hurt." For context on the September 11 terrorist attacks and the Iraq War, I relied on Jon Lee Anderson's *The Fall of Baghdad*, Seymour Hersh's *Chain of Command: The Road from 9/11 to Abu Ghraib*, Christopher Cerf and Micha L. Sifry's *The Iraq War Reader: History, Documents, Opinions*, Lawrence Wright's *The Looming Tower: Al Qaeda and the Road to 9/11*, and others. And for background on Israel, the intifada, and the Holocaust, I referred to Meron Benvenisti's *Intimate Enemies: Jews and Arabs in a Shared Land*, Thomas Friedman's *From Beirut to Jerusalem*, Joost Hiltermann's *Behind the Intifada: Labor and Women's Movements in the Occupied Territories*, Barnet Litvinoff's *The Burning Bush: Anti-Semitism and World History*, Edward Said's *From Oslo to Iraq and the Roadmap*, and Elie Wiesel's *Night*, and others.